THE
ZIONIST
DREAM
REVISITED

THE ZIONIST DREAM REVISITED

From Herzl to Gush Emunim
and Back

AMNON RUBINSTEIN

SCHOCKEN BOOKS • NEW YORK

First published by Schocken Books 1984
10 9 8 7 6 5 4 3 2 1   84 85 86 87
Copyright © 1984 by Amnon Rubinstein
Originally published as *Me-Hertsel ad Gush emunim ya-hazarah* by Schocken
Ltd., Tel Aviv

Library of Congress Cataloging in Publication Data
Rubinstein, Amnon.
  The Zionist dream revisited.
  Translation of: Me-Hertsel ad Gush emunim ya-hazarah.
  Includes bibliographical references and index.
  1. Israel—Politics and government. 2. Jews—Identity. 3. Zionism. ·4.
National characteristics, Israeli. 5. Judaism—Israel. I. Title.
DS126.5.R84513 1984   956.94′001   83–20245

Designed by Nancy Dale Muldoon
Manufactured in the United States of America
ISBN 0-8052-3886-7

To Roni, Tal, and Nir

CONTENTS

Preface

LEBANON AND THE BURDEN OF JEWISH HISTORY

In June 1982, Israeli forces marched into southern Lebanon, and thus opened a new chapter in the history of the Jewish state. The war and its aftermath highlighted Israel's twin crises: a growing polarization at home compounded by increasing isolation, verging on ostracism, in the world community.

The war involved the bombing of civilian towns in which the PLO had rooted itself and culminated with the siege of Beirut. When, in September 1982, news of the massacre perpetrated by the Maronite phalangists in the Palestinian refugee camps of Sabra and Shatilla descended upon a stunned Israel, the country had already been torn apart by an unprecedented schism.

For the first time in Israel's history, the nation went to war without the customary national consensus. The sounds of war were thus intermingled with the voices of dissent. While overhead the airplanes could be heard on their routine sorties, the meetings and demonstrations gathered momentum. The vast Kings of Israel Square in central Tel Aviv became the scene of alternate mass rallies, supporting or denouncing the war. The army, made up as it is of draftees and reservists, mirrored this debate, and Israelis at home could watch their own doubts and dissensions articulated by soldiers facing the television camera. While the majority supported former Prime Minister Menachem Begin's initial move, a substantial minority uttered its disagreement in loud and harsh terms. Soldiers and officers

signed petitions refusing to serve in Lebanon, a few radicals
even preferred defiance and jail to obeying orders. The debate
was couched mainly in political terms. Begin and his followers
admitted that the incursion into Lebanon was an initiated
move—as distinct from Israel's traditional "no-choice" wars—
but defended it on grounds of both justice and expedience. The
opposition retorted by pointing to the heavy price Israel would
pay in blood and political standing for the venture and to the
danger of splitting the nation on the one issue which should
have remained above domestic disputes.

But behind this exchange lurks another dimension: Never
has a war been so debated in purely Jewish—as distinct from
Israeli—terms. Begin justified the war and the cruelty inflicted
upon the civilian population by invoking repeatedly images
and memories of World War II and the Holocaust. What the
Syrians were doing before the war to the Christians was "exactly" what the Germans had done to Jews in the forties, and
Israel was not going to let this happen. The bombing of Beirut
was akin to the bombing of German cities—Dresden was the
unfortunate precedent mentioned by the prime minister—and
the PLO were equated with the Nazis. The prime minister, in a
speech delivered to the National Security College, in mid-
August, defended the Israeli initiative by referring again and
again to the history of Nazi aggression which went unchecked
until finally a "no-choice" war was forced upon Britain and
France and, eventually, upon Stalin's Soviet Union: "World
War II really began on March 7, 1936, when Hitler sent two
German battalions into the demilitarized Rhineland. At that
time, two French divisions could have marched in and turned
the invaders into prisoners of war and thereby toppled Hitler."[1]
But the West did not believe in initiating wars—even one that
could have been easily won. Consequently, it later had to wage
a most costly and dreadful war in which millions of people and
a third of the Jews perished. Operation Peace of Galilee, added
Begin, was not a "no-choice" war. "The terrorists did not menace the existence of Israel; they 'only' threatened the lives of

Israelis and the Jews." Israel was not going to repeat the mistakes of the free world facing the Nazi aggression but would do what France and Britain should have done in 1936.

In his letter to President Ronald Reagan, dated August 2, 1982, in the midst of the siege of Beirut, Begin reverted again—in what must be regarded as an overstatement—to the familiar analogy:

May I tell you, dear Mr. President, how I feel these days when I turn to the Creator of my soul in deep gratitude: I feel as a prime minister empowered to instruct a valiant army facing "Berlin" where, amongst innocent civilians, Hitler and his henchmen hide in a bunker deep beneath the surface.[2]

And when the news of the massacre in Sabra and Shatilla brought a strong condemnation of Israel, Begin again invoked the dormant memories of Jewish history: He labeled this outcry a "blood libel" alleging that, as in the past, "goyim kill goyim and they want to blame the Jews." In his response to Senator Alan Cranston's expression of deep concern over Israel's behavior in Lebanon, the Prime Minister wrote on September 29, 1982:

The whole campaign of the last ten days of accusing Israel, of blaming Israel, of placing moral responsibility on Israel—all of it seems to me, an old man who has seen so much in his lifetime—to be almost unbelievable, fantastic and, of course, totally despicable. Observing this behavior I cannot help but remember that in Jewish history, leveling false accusations is a repeated feature of our own experience. It is almost inexplicable but true, the astonishing fact—Jews condemned as the poisoners of wells, the killers of Christian children for the Pesach ritual, the spreaders of the Black Plague—and with what not. And now this.[3]

But this constant reliance on Jewish history, this repeated reference to World War II and the Holocaust, this feverish determination to set past wrongs right through Israel's might was merely one aspect of the national debate. To the opponents of the government, another, totally different lesson had to be elic-

ited from the Jewish experience. War could only be justified in
a clear case of self-defense. The bombing of Beirut was offensive and objectionable because it violated Jewish tenets. Biblical injunctions were cited by the two opposing camps: While
the nationalist-religious zealots of Gush Emunim laid claim to
the whole of southern Lebanon as being God-given to the tribe
of Asher, other religious figures raised a courageous voice
against the Israeli action. While Gush activists invoked the
commandment to eradicate the Amalekites, some religious
voices of moderation denounced the bombing of Beirut by referring to the patriarch Abraham pleading with God to spare
Sodom for the sake of even one solitary righteous person.
Heading a small protest movement of reservists, Abraham
Burg, who volunteered to join his unit despite a disability
caused in a previous war, directed a public question at Prime
Minister Begin: Would he have ordered the raids on Beirut had
a Jewish community been there? Burg, the son of the minister
of the interior in Begin's cabinet, became famous overnight,
but his question remained unanswered, and he continued to
assail the government. As Jews, he claimed, we are bound to
hold that each man is made in God's image and just as we
would have avoided bombing Beirut in order to save the lives of
Jews so must we act in order to spare the lives of the innocent
regardless of their nationality and religion.

Outside the religious camp, opposition to the government's
policy reached a new pitch of denunciation among the more
radical elements. Here, too, Jewish history was mobilized to
scourge Begin and Ariel Sharon, the then Minister of Defense—
and the Holocaust was again invoked. But the victims now
were not the Jews; they were the Palestinians. Hebrew University professors, as well as Knesset members and journalists,
railed against the prime minister's belittling and cheapening
the memory of the slaughtered six million by attaching the
terms "Hitlerite" and "Nazi" to Arafat and the PLO. Yad
Vashem, the Holocaust memorial in Jerusalem, soon became

the focal point of a national controversy. Next to its gate, a survivor of the Warsaw Ghetto and Buchenwald staged a hunger strike against Begin's policy. The father of a paratrooper, he issued a public statement:

When I was a child of ten and was liberated from the concentration camp, I thought that we shall never suffer again. I did not dream that we could cause suffering to others. Today we are doing just that. The Germans in Buchenwald starved us to death. Today, in Jerusalem, I starve myself, and this hunger of mine is no less horrific. When I hear "filthy Arabs" I remember "filthy Jews." I see Beirut and I remember Warsaw.[4]

In a conference organized by Yad Vashem, a young Israeli-born woman, who was a member of the panel, protested against Begin's invoking the Holocaust and drew parallels between the persecution of the Jews and the lot of the Palestinians. She was quickly ruled out of order by her scandalized colleagues, but the storm spilled over to the press. The then Chief of Staff, General Rafael Eytan, ordered the cessation of all army visits to Yad Vashem because he regarded remarks by one of the young guides, an outspoken opponent of the war in Lebanon, as unpatriotic. He told the soldiers that there was no difference between perishing in the gas chambers of Auschwitz and dying in a burning Merkavah tank in Lebanon. A bereaved father, who lost his only son in Lebanon, addressed the government in the following words:

I, remnant of a rabbinical family, only son of my father, a Zionist and a Socialist, who died a hero's death in the Warsaw Ghetto revolt, survived the Holocaust and settled in our country and served in the army and married and had a son. Now my beloved son is dead because of your war. Thus you have discontinued a Jewish chain of age-old suffering generations which no persecutor has succeeded in severing. The history of our ancient, wise and racked people will judge and punish you with whips and scorpions, and let my sorrow haunt you when you sleep and when you wake up, and let my grief be the Mark of Cain on your forehead forever![5]

In the wake of the massacre in Sabra and Shatilla the tenor of the attacks against Begin and Sharon became more strident and more accusatory. A young poet, Zvi Atzmon, gave this mood an eloquent expression. In a poem called *Yizkor*—the Jewish prayer in memory of the dead—he recounted in short, factual statements the singular record of persecution, martyrdom, and murder of the Jews throughout the ages. Then, when "there had already been, if you will, a legend's hope" of Zionist revival, the Jews were "starved and poisoned and butchered and hanged and buried alive and burnt and torn apart, and let the revenge of a slaughtered small child cry out."[6] Then, suddenly, the Jewish people get up in the morning and "see children shot while the sun shone"—a reference to Chaim Nachman Bialik's famous poem about the Kishinev pogroms of 1905—"and real blood, this week—this is no libel—of Arab children." And the poet concluded:

> In Eretz Israel arose the Jewish people,
> laden with all its history, two thousand years old,
> and as long as there is inside my heart a soul:
> I am guilty.

Needless to say, this extreme mood is shared only by a small minority, but the magnitude of the moral outrage felt by Israelis after the massacre drew an estimated 400,000 into the Kings of Israel Square and forced a reluctant Menachem Begin to change his mind and establish a judicial inquiry of the massacre, a demand he had rejected only a few days before.

When the commission of inquiry, headed by the president of the Supreme Court, Justice Yitzchak Kahan, rendered its report in February 1983, it established a new norm of conduct by placing upon army officers and political leaders a hitherto unprecedented legal duty to actively protect a civilian population—even an alien population—from the effects of their decisions. In drawing such far-reaching conclusions, the commission invoked a lesson from Jewish history:

When we are dealing with the issue of indirect responsibility, it should also not be forgotten that the Jews in various lands of exile, and also in the Land of Israel when it was under foreign rule, suffered greatly from pogroms perpetrated by various hooligans; and the danger of disturbances against Jews in various lands, it seems evident, has not yet passed. The Jewish public's stand has always been that the responsibility for such deeds falls not only on those who rioted and committed the atrocities but also on those who were responsible for safety and public order, who could have prevented the disturbances and did not fulfill their obligations in this respect. It is true that the regimes of various countries, among them even enlightened countries, have sidestepped such responsibility on more than one occasion and have not established inquiry commissions to investigate the issue of indirect responsibility, such as we are speaking about; but the development of ethical norms in the world public requires that the approach to this issue be universally shared and that the responsibility be placed not just on the perpetrators but also on those who could and should have prevented the commission of those deeds which must be condemned.[7]

The report was not accepted unanimously by Israeli public opinion, and Ariel Sharon—ousted from the Ministry of Defense in the wake of the report—lashed out against it. In public opinion polls, about 50 percent supported the committee; over 30 percent rejected it as totally unacceptable. However, the national debate which emerged from the Lebanese venture should not be measured by headcounts and political results. The very soul of Israel was at stake and the very purpose of Zionism was being questioned. The burden of Jewish history, and the contradictory lessons to be drawn from it, have thus acquired a pressing relevance. And this relevance has deepened and been exacerbated by events outside the country.

Israel's war in Lebanon—which, at least originally, had a legitimate and justifiable *casus*—became a highly visible and strongly criticized event. As distinct from remote, untelevised wars, the suffering and carnage wreaked upon the Lebanese was brought home with the nightly newscasts to hundreds of millions of horrified spectators. As the war dragged on and the siege of Beirut became nasty, criticism of Israel grew into vociferous

accusations. Israel, accustomed to being the target of international rebuke, was on the point of becoming an ostracized leper.
In successive votes at the United Nations, the disparate members of the General Assembly forsook their traditional animosi-
ties and, with the sole exception of the United States, united in
routine condemnations of Israel's behavior. Time after time,
Israel found itself in the dock facing an infuriated international
jury. With the events in Sabra and Shatilla, the shrill voices
turned into a hysterical chorus. The Maronite perpetrators of
the atrocities were passed over, unnoticed and uncensored—
President Amin Gemayel was widely cheered and applauded in
the United Nations—but Israelis were denounced in unprecedented terms. Afghanistan and Cambodia continued to sink
into the limbo of marginal and nontelevisable news as all attention was focused on one villain: the Jewish state. The people
who only fifteen years before had won a war and the world's
admiration in those famous six days of June 1967 were transformed into the target of unremittent hostility. Within a rela-
tively short time, Israel's image underwent a drastic metamorphosis—from darling to knave, from David to Goliath.

Indeed, the anti-Israeli mood reached such heights that the
Israeli action in Lebanon has continuously been compared
with Nazi atrocities. Writing from Washington for the London
Spectator, Nickolas von Hoffman asserted that "incident by
incident, atrocity by atrocity, Americans are coming to see the
Israeli government pounding the Star of David into a swas-
tika."[8] In scores of cartoons appearing in the European press,
Prime Minister Begin was depicted as a Jewish Hitler and the
Palestinians as the butchered Jews. Anti-Israeli slogans and
graffiti spread through many European cities, and for a while it
seemed as if southern Lebanon was the only spot on earth
where blood was being shed and that only Israel was engaged in
war operations.

In the wake of the events in Lebanon, a new wave of anti-
Semitism swept over Europe—an unwelcome ghost materializ-
ing from the ostensibly buried past. The European office of the

Anti-Defamation League counted at least fifty-five incidents of anti-Semitism in thirteen European countries during June, July, and August 1982:

It was pointed out that the list is by no means exhaustive because many acts of anti-Jewish vandalism and violence go unreported and unrecorded. Not included in the fifty-five incidents was the large number of threatening telephone calls and letters received by Jewish leaders and institutions in the aftermath of Israel's entry into Lebanon on June 6.[9]

Extreme left and extreme right united in an unholy alliance in order to attack the remnant of the Jews living in Europe. Bombing and machine-gunning of Jews in Paris and Rome drew public attention to the seriousness of the new onslaught. Jews in synagogues and community centers were forced to resort to unprecedented precautions. The chief rabbi of Britain, following police advice, did not venture out without a bulletproof vest; in traditionally pro-Jewish Amsterdam, a conference on Zionism and anti-Semitism had to take place under heavy police protection. The Brussels Conference on Soviet Jewry, scheduled to take place in Paris in October 1982, was moved to Jerusalem because of "a hostile climate." Even in Australia—where Jews had never been exposed to serious anti-Semitic incidents—the old-new plague struck: In January 1983 two bombs exploded at the Melbourne Jewish Center, and shots were fired at a religious Zionist youth camp. Threatening phone calls warned that the attacks would continue unless Israel withdrew from Lebanon.

Australia was not a solitary case. In Scandinavia and in other countries with no anti-Jewish tradition, such as Italy and Greece, the symptoms of the plague began to appear. In Greece, a blatant anti-Israeli and anti-Jewish campaign was permitted by Mr. Papandreou's government and soon reached alarming dimensions. In addition to the traditional graffiti telling the Jews to "go home"—wherever that may be—the fiery articles and the denunciation of Israel as "worse than the Nazis, more hateful than Hitler," open threats were directed at Jewish establishments, and the state-controlled radio went so far as to read a call for the boycott of Jewish businessmen. The fury of the Greek press—one journal warned foreign Jewish artists and athletes not to visit Greece—was particularly strange. Israel's allies in Lebanon were, after all, Christian, and its staunchest friend, Major Saad Haddad, is a Greek Catholic: Yet in a country with no virulent anti-Semitic tradition, the fury against Israel was coupled with attacks on Jews in general. These outbursts became so alarming that over one hundred Greek intellectuals and scientists published a special petition warning against this "new climate of antisemitism." While condemning the invasion of Lebanon, the petition argued against identifying Jews (Israelites) with Israelis or with Israel, Zionism, and "the murderous policy of Begin and Sharon."[10]

In Israel itself, this frightening, all-too-familiar specter became another demonstration that "the world" was inherently and remorselessly against the Jews and that objections to the policies of the Jewish State were not a valid criticism but merely another manifestation of the old disease. Mr. Begin's Likud party seized upon these events as self-fulfilling evidence of the rightness of its cause. "We can't do right anyway, so let's do what we ought to do regardless of what others say"—ran a common sentiment. But other voices in opposition could be heard. The government was held responsible for not taking into account the impact of its actions on a sensitive Diaspora. Others pointed out that it would be misleading and dangerous to sink into a self-righteous mood which automatically equates anti-Semitism with harsh criticism of Israel. As Uriel Tal, professor of Jewish history at Tel Aviv University, pointed out, a pro-Palestinian sentiment often emanates from the very same groups who have supported Israel in the past and who are in the forefront of the struggle against anti-Semitism. Events in the Diaspora thus fanned the flames of the ongoing internal debate. Israel, virtually ostracized, was being shattered by bitter dissension from within.

But the war in Lebanon and its aftermath highlighted a deeper tragic paradox: Here was mighty Israel, which by the efficiency of its war machine had become the very antithesis of the traditionally helpless Jew, reverting to that historical role from which Zionism was supposed to save the Jews; here was a reborn Judea forcibly cloaked with an image against which the Zionist founders railed and rebelled; here was the Zionist dream come true, the Jewish state, which had sought to become a normal member of the family of nations, turning into an international pariah; and, worse still, here was the Zionist dream come true—the state which was conceived by Herzl not only as a shelter for a homeless people but also as the state that would liberate the Christian world from anti-Semitism—serving as the ostensible cause for the reappearance of the old malignancy.

What happened to that Zionist dream?

What went wrong?

It is with these questions that this book attempts to grapple.

THE
ZIONIST
DREAM
REVISITED

1

ZIONISM AND THE QUEST FOR A NEW JEWISH IDENTITY

In 1905, after Dr. Theodor Herzl's sudden death, a stunned grief descended upon the fledgling Zionist organization, moving a young Russian Jew to publish an obituary commemorating the founder of Zionism. Years later, that young man, Vladimir Jabotinsky, would acquire some posthumous international fame as the original teacher and mentor of former Israeli Prime Minister Menachem Begin. But, at the time, Jabotinsky was one of many young and ardent Russian Jews whose conversion to Zionism manifested itself in a total attachment to Herzl.

Not content with cliché eulogies or mere charisma, Jabotinsky, in his obituary, tried to explain the unique impact that the author of *Die Judenstaat* had on the Jews. The all-consuming adoration, the total subjugation to Herzl's personality could not be explained in ordinary political terms.

According to Jabotinsky, Herzl's importance was related to the inherent difficulty accompanying the birth of the new nation Zionism sought to bring about. The difficulty lay in the fact that this new type of Jew was unknown to any of the Zionist founders. "A nation, which lives a normal national life on its land," wrote Jabotinsky, "is replete with stereotypes representing a characteristic national image."[1] Among the nations of the earth are types immediately recognizable as typically Russian, or English, or German. But, with us, continued Jabotinsky, there is no such characteristic type. "What we see around us among Jews is merely the outcome of arbitrary action perpetrated by others." This prevalent Jew, the *Yid*, as he is pejoratively called by the Gentiles, does not reflect the proud national past but embodies the very negative traits from which Zionism seeks to redeem the Jews. "Only after removing the dust accumulated through two thousand years of exile, of *galut*, will the true, authentic Hebrew character reveal its glorious head. Only then shall we be able to say: This is a typical Hebrew, in every sense of the word."

In the meantime, the portrait of such a future Hebrew cannot be visualized but merely deduced by juxtaposing him against the prevalent diaspora Jew. The words Jabotinsky used are incisive:

Our starting point is to take the typical Yid of today and to imagine his diametrical opposite . . . because the Yid is ugly, sickly, and lacks decorum, we shall endow the ideal image of the Hebrew with masculine beauty. The Yid is trodden upon and easily frightened and, therefore, the Hebrew ought to be proud and independent. The Yid is despised by all and, therefore, the Hebrew ought to charm all. The Yid has accepted submission and, therefore, the Hebrew ought to learn how to command. The Yid wants to conceal his identity from strangers and, therefore, the Hebrew should look the world straight in the eye and declare: "I am a Hebrew!"

Such a liberated Jew, such a future Hebrew, explained Jabotinsky, was Theodor Herzl. His personality, his demeanor, his majestic appearance embodied everything which Jews were not but sought to be. It was this element which struck such a strong chord in the collective Jewish mind and which explained why Herzl's death sent such deep shock waves throughout the Jewish world.

Sixty-five years after the publication of this obituary, in 1955, a research project was undertaken at Tel Aviv University dealing with the self-image of secondary school Israeli students. The publication of the resulting paper caused some public stir, but it actually confirmed a commonly held suspicion: The young Israeli, the Sabra, imputes to himself positive traits which are diametrically contrasted, almost instinctively, with imputed negative traits of the Jew in Exile, the old diaspora Jew.

The Sabras, when describing themselves, use many of Jabotinsky's adjectives: tall, strong and hardy, tanned and freckled, dynamic, ill-mannered, patriotic, free, pioneering, impudent and good-hearted, arrogant and well-liked. On the other hand, the diaspora Jew is pale and thin, weak and sickly, frightened and distrustful; he lacks self-confidence and is sad, shy and perplexed, taciturn and polite. In short, the Sabra is the positive; the diaspora Jew the negative.

Along this historical line, from Jabotinsky's glorification of the new-Jew-to-come to the self-image of the new Jew incarnate, there are a multitude of similar juxtapositions. Zionist literature abounds with this very posture: the old-time Jew contrasted with the newly born Hebrew; the exile Jew with the native Sabra; the Yid of yesteryear with the resurrected Maccabees; the inferior Jew with the super Jew.

The message was loud and clear: The Hebrew, the new super Jew, represents everything which has traditionally been associated with the Gentiles, the goyim, the other side; while the dominant traits of the diaspora Jew—our "miserable stepbrother," to use David Ben Gurion's phrase—were to be discarded.

Reading today—in a post-Holocaust era—the writings of the founders of Zionism, one is slightly embarrassed by the abuse against the very nature of Jewish communities in exile, in galut. Their poverty is reviled, their helplessness despised, their virtues ignored.

Zionism did not usher in this mood. Nineteenth-century Hebrew and Yiddish literature—the first manifestations of a nonreligious Jewish culture in Eastern Europe—vilify the Jewish existence within the traditional Pale of Settlement, the "parasitical" occupations which mar it and the sickening submission to brute force and oppression. Zionism, especially in Eastern Europe, was founded upon this total rejection of Jewish existence in galut but, unlike its forerunners, indicated a way out. Zionism is not content with returning the Jewish people to its lost sovereignty and never-forgotten homeland; it also seeks to be the midwife who helps the Jewish people give birth to a new kind of man. This revolution—no less than the political craving for independence—is the very basis of Zionist philosophy and explains its seeming paradoxes. Yes, the Jews are despised and lead an inferior life; no, it is not their inherent fault, as the anti-Semites charge: Circumstance alone is responsible for their plight. Thus Nachman Syrkin, one of the founding ideologists of the Zionist Labor movement, wrote: "Puny, ugly, enslaved, degraded and egoistic is the Jew when he forgets his great self; great, beautiful, moral and social is the Jew when he returns to himself and recognizes his own soul."[2]

Normality means this redemption of the individual as well as the normalization of the people. The Return to Zion is coupled with a metamorphosis of the Jew into a new man. The Jew would become a "goy" in the double meaning that this word has in Hebrew, signifying both "gentile"and "nation." Once this rebirth takes place, the traumas of the past will have been forgotten. To be a goy means to be healthy; healthy nations, healthy people are not obsessed with issues of existence and survival. Moshe Leib Lilienblum, one of the founders of the pre-Herzlian "Lovers of Zion" movement in Russia, indicated the dimensions of this transition: If the Jews are going to be a normal goy, they should know how such normal goyim behave:

Mixed marriages and foreign culture are not strange to a healthy people. Such people swallow everything and digest everything. And occasionally, the foreign things they take in, turn into a source of life. A healthy people are oblivious to the fear of death and do not have to be on guard in order to ensure their survival.[3]

"To be a goy" was, therefore, the dominant theme of Zionist philosophy in its formative period. The idea was so forceful that it united the warring factions and parties. On everything else Zionists differed: "Territorialists," who were ready to consider territories outside Palestine as a "night shelter" for the hard-pressed Jews, clashed with "Zionists of Zion," who regarded any substitute to the ancestral homeland—including the notorious British offer to settle Jewish refugees in Uganda—as high treason; "practical Zionists," who believed in practical steps to implement Zionism, railed against those who believed mainly in political and international action; Labor Zionists, who saw the return to Zion inextricably intertwined with a socialist-universal mission, fought against the Zionist Right, which gave precedence to the national cause. Even the very basic idea of a Jewish state did not escape dispute and much doubt was cast on its soundness and practicality. One idea—rather one craving, one urge—enjoyed a veritable consensus: to be a new people; to escape the role which history imposed on the Jews; to become, in Herzl's words, "a wondrous breed of Jews which will spring up from the earth."[4]

Indeed, Jewish existence in exile was regarded as lying outside history. Both Ben Gurion and Jabotinsky, incorrigible opponents, denied the legitimacy of Jewish history in galut. Ben-Gurion said:

Since our last national tragedy—the suppression of the Bar Kochba rebellion by the Romans—we have had "histories" of persecution, of legal discrimination, of the Inquisition and the pogroms, of dedication and martyrdom, but we did not have Jewish history anymore, because a history of a people is only what the people create as a whole, as a national unit, and not the sum total of what happens to individuals and to groups within the people. For the last fifteen hundred years, we have been excluded from world history which is made up of the histories of peoples.[5]

Even the religious Zionists, aware as they were of the historic continuity which gave a meaning to Jewish survival even in exile, subscribed to these extreme sentiments. Thus S. H. Landau, founder of *Hapoel Hamizrachi,* the religious labor movement which gave rise to the National Religious Party, wrote:

Israel in exile ceased to be a people or, to be exact, a living people. . . . A people lacking a land of their own whose natural life force has dried up is not a people. Parasitism, conscious or unconscious, becomes its second nature—parasitism of the individual and of the community.[6]

This was the driving power behind the Zionist call for a total revolt—against passivity, against tradition, against all which, at the time, was synonymous with Jewishness.

But in addition to this Zionist consensus there was a deep division regarding the very essence of the new Jewish society to be created in Palestine. This division demonstrated the difference between the Jews who came into Zionism via the route of a failed emancipation and the Jewish communities of Eastern Europe living under the yoke of an authoritarian Czarist regime, from which emancipation was conspicuously absent.

Herzl himself personified this chasm between East and West. His attachment to Judaism was minimal; his knowledge of things Jewish nebulous, consisting mainly of childhood memories of a Budapest synagogue. As a European, as a civilized man, anti-Semitism aroused in him anger and disgust. When he gradually came to discover the unfathomable depth and intensity of the new-old sickness, he was driven to the idea of a Jewish state. Yet, his very philosophy remained European, secular, and liberal. He sought to heal the ugly wound which afflicted the Jews and marred the enlightened face of Christian Europe: hence, his stubborn insistence on the need for international recognition and cooperation with enlightened Gentiles in carrying out the Return to Zion. That recognition, Herzl argued, should be expressed through a charter enabling the Jews to return to their homeland. The granting of the charter by the enlightened nations of Europe would constitute the one event revolutionizing relations between Jews and Gentiles. The creation of a Jewish commonwealth, a progressive society based on the European model, would symbolize the end of anti-Semitism. Recognition is imperative not only because of obvious demands of political expediency but also because of the need to put an end to the tragic friction between Jews and Christians.

Because assimilation was impossible and did not solve the issue of a Jewish existence in an antagonistic Christian environment, Herzl rejected its very notion:

We have sincerely tried everywhere to merge with the national communities in which we live, seeking only to preserve the faith of our fathers. It is not permitted us. In vain we are loyal patriots, sometimes superloyal; in vain do we make the same sacrifices of life and property as our fellow citizens; in vain do we strive to enhance the fame of our native lands in the arts and sciences or their wealth by trade and commerce. In our native lands where we have lived for centuries we are still decried as aliens, often by men whose ancestors had not yet come at a time when Jewish sighs had long been heard in the country. The majority decide who the "alien" is; this, and all else in the relations between peoples, is a matter of power.[7]

In this respect, Herzl was a spokesman for a whole generation of acculturated, assimilated Jews who found their way to Jewish nationalism. With him, as with other founders of Zionism, anti-Semitism was the prime mover; but as soon as the urge to combat it took the form of a national solution, a new pride in their half-forgotten, vaguely sensed, Jewish heritage set in.

This pride notwithstanding, there was precious little Jewishness in Herzl's writings. The new Maccabees who would inhabit the utopian future state were not really different from the cultivated European—that figure of reason and progress whose love and acceptance Jews like Herzl sought in vain.

Herzl's colleague in the First Zionist Congress, Max Nordau, shared these attitudes. Nordau himself was a product of Jewish assimilation. Before his conversion by Herzl to Zionism, he had already acquired a reputation throughout Europe as an atheist thinker, an iconoclast author, and a sharp critic of European manners and morals. Like Herzl, his education was basically Germanic, his outlook cosmopolitan. Like Herzl, he lost contact with Judaism, and like him he watched with shock the old anti-Semitic monster raise its menacing head. Like Herzl, his new attachment to Jewish nationalism was neither motivated, nor accompanied, by a return to Judaism. In his moving address to the First Zionist Congress in Basel in 1897, he described the plight of the emancipated western Jews—talented, ready to serve their beloved countries, humiliated, and rejected by their Christian neighbors. This plight, Nordau stressed, should not be an exclusively Jewish concern:

To Jewish distress no one can remain indifferent—neither Christian nor Jew. It is a great sin to let a race, whose ability even its worst enemies do not deny, degenerate into intellectual and physical misery. It is a sin against them and it is a sin against the course of civilization, to whose progress Jews have made, and will yet make, significant contributions.[8]

For Herzl and Nordau, anti-Semitism was a plague affecting both Jew and Gentile, but it also explained where the evil was and how it could be uprooted. For the Jews, it served as a reminder of their unique position: They shared not merely a common faith but also a common fate. Herzl's conclusion— "we are a people—one people"—was totally realistic: "Prosperity weakens us as Jews and wipes out our differences; only pressure drives us back to our own; only hostility stamps us ever again as strangers."

Willingly or unwillingly, the Jews remain one: "Affliction binds us togther, and, thus united, we suddenly discover our strength."

Upon this diagnosis, Herzl wrote his prescription for the Jewish illness, and his remedy is captivating in its simplicity: The new Jews will establish an exemplary society characterized by tolerance and social justice, and they shall not forget "the ways of the world." They shall acquire the same international habits and customs which enable the world to have "English hotels in Egypt and on Swiss mountain tops, Viennese cafés in South Africa, French theaters in Russia, German operas in America, and the world's best Bavarian beer in Paris."[9]

The Jews, in short, will finally become true Europeans. They shall, for instance, forsake the peddlers' trade which has so infuriated the anti-Semites. Herzl did not rebel against these anti-Semitic labels. Modern European experience proves, he wrote in *Die Judenstaat*, that through modern marketing techniques and department stores, it is possible to prevent in the future Jewish state the renewal of the hated Jewish trades. Thus the Jews' own state would rid both Europe and the Jews of their problems. The Jews will be able to occupy all appropriate trades and professions without enraging their threatened Christian rivals. They shall settle on the land and cultivate it without bringing upon them the wrath of the Christian farmer, without the envy and antagonism which frustrated all attempts to turn Jews into farmers in Europe. The state of the Jews will therefore be a mini-Switzerland in the heart of the Middle East. It will be, as Herzl entitled his famous booklet *Die Judenstaat*, a state of the Jews, hardly a Jewish state.

In Herzl's utopian novel, *Altneuland*, which depicts an imaginary journey to the new state, as well as in the Zionist writings of Max Nordau, who did not forsake his militant atheism upon his conversion to Zionism, the recurrent theme is the integration of the Jew into western civilization. Since he was barred from entrance to this world through emancipation and tolerance, he shall enter it through the new gate: full participation founded not on a personal but on a national, sovereign equality.

In the European fin de siècle political climate, the renewal of Jewish political independence seemed—certainly to western Zionists—the embodiment of the spirit of modernity and progress. Anti-Semitism is criminal because, among other evils, it precludes the Jews from participating in, and contributing to, a progressive western society. Their immigration to a territory of their own, in which their national identity combines with a liberal progressive spirit, would remove this obstacle.

This analysis throws light on the universal nature of the Herzlian approach: The establishment of a state for the Jews and their emigration out of Europe were compatible with the interests of the family of enlightened nations. The western world would rid itself of a painful problem and would acquire another civilized offshoot state which would incorporate its highest values. Zionism is not only a Jewish revolution; it is, to quote Herzl, "simply the peacemaker"; it proclaims peace between Jews and Gentiles, between Judaism and Christianity.

It is, of course, easy to deride, with the benefit of hindsight, such simplistic attitudes and to criticize Herzl and many of his colleagues for failing to appreciate the enduring vigor of traditional Jewish civilization and to fathom the depths of those ancient roots which nourish anti-Semitism. Indeed, as we shall see, such criticism was leveled at Herzl at the time by other Zionists. Nevertheless, it was this very simplistic attitude—a product of a European non-Jewish environment—which translated into political action the age-old yearning for Zion and which forged an organizational tool destined to save many Jews from persecution and extinction.

Herzl's declaration that the Jews are a people, that there is an international interest in giving them a land of their own, and that Zionism offered a total solution to both Jews and Gentiles was responsible for taking Zionist ideas out of the amateurish circles of the "Lovers of Zion" movement and placing them squarely in the focal center of Jewish and international attention. Without such a simplistic attitude—again, typically non-Jewish—without couching the Jewish problem in universal and international terms, it is doubtful whether a Zionist movement would have been established or whether massive Jewish immigration into Palestine would have replaced the trickle of pious Jews and devoted pioneers which preceded Herzl's initiative.

However, Herzl's and Nordau's idea of what "normalization" meant did not pass unchallenged. His secular, western concept of the new Jewish society was anathema to many who were unwilling or unable to forsake what they regarded as their Jewish raison d'être.

Herzl's most awesome opponent was the Hebrew author Asher Zvi Ginsberg, who, under the pen name Ahad Ha'am, periodically delivered literary broadsides against the west europeanized concept of Jewish nationalism. In a series of vitriolic critiques, Ahad Ha'am demolished Herzl's *Altneuland:* "Anyone examining this book will find that in their state the Jews have neither renewed nor added anything of their own. Only what they saw fragmented among the enlightened nations of Europe and America, they imitated and put together in their new land." And Ahad Ha'am added sardonically that Herzl denied the Jews even the credit for uniting these fragments into a new whole; even that art was a result of circumstance, not talent; because they founded their state without "the agony of heritage," they were in a position to pick and choose the best from everywhere—because, as Herzl put it, they were especially qualified for this task by their economic and cosmopolitan expertise.[10]

This typical clash between Herzl and Ahad Ha'am reflected, to a large extent, the wide divergence between the emancipated western Jews who entered Zionism via the corridor of frustrated assimilation and the Jewish masses of Eastern Europe living under the authoritarian yoke of antisemitic regimes. In western Europe, Jews experienced, for a short time, the sweet taste of equal rights; they participated in the seemingly rational and secular new era with an eagerness fed by generations of cultural deprivation. In the East, masses of impoverished Jews lived in their crowded Pale of Settlement isolation, subject to perennial persecution and periodic violence.

In the West, a great part of the Jews shook themselves free of the Jewish tradition which shaped their forefathers' world. They sought to obliterate their former "otherness" and merge into the host societies through secularization, assimilation, reform synagogues, intermarriage, and conversion. The speed with which they acted—within one or two generations they had moved from ghettos to the very heart of European civilization—attested to their urge to cast off the yoke of a tradition which many regarded as irrelevant in the new era of progress and enlightenment.

In the East, too, the ghetto walls were beginning to crack. The vast majority of Jews living in Poland, czarist Russia, and Rumania belonged to Yiddish-speaking, Orthodox, and self-contained communities. But there were the Maskilim—the enlightened and secularized men of letters—and there was even some initial Jewish response to a half-hearted czarist attempt at Russification of the Jews. There were the few who broke through the Pale of Settlement into Russian society and acquired "non-Jewish" professions. There was some hope of a better, more progressive Russia, and there was, of course, a growing rebellion among the young against the Jewish Orthodox establishment. The emergence of a new Jewish proletariat and the opening up of some secular schools to Jews ushered in a sense of an impending turning point which would bring Russia closer to western standards. Instead, Russia reverted to a series of pogroms, beginning in 1881 after the assassination of Czar Alexander II, which ended any hope that the czarist regime would emulate the West in granting some measure of equal rights to the Jews.

Thus, eastern Jews witnessed a rejection similar in some respects—yet more brutal and violent—to what drove Herzl and other western Jews toward Zionism. In both parts of Europe, the Jewish intelligentsia encountered a double rejection: the traditional, boorish anti-Semitism was compounded and made more horrible by the acquiescence of the intellectuals in the West and the socialist revolutionaries in the East. But in the East, the rejection was inherently different from that which came to be associated with the Dreyfus affair in the West. For the Jewish communities of Russia, Poland, and Rumania—the great bulk of Jews from which Zionism would draw its main strength—emancipation was a distant dream but Judaism was a present, palpable reality. For the East European Zionists, the synagogue was not a vague memory of childhood days but a reality against which they rebelled. Jewish culture, with its rich tradition of prayers and folklore, was familiar. The Hebrew language did not sound strange and foreign. Many learned it as the language of the new Jews. Yiddish was spoken by almost all. As well as being their ancestral homeland, *Eretz Israel* (the Land of Israel) was familiar from the Bible, the prayer book, and the fledgling Hebrew literature.

For the East European Zionist, Judaism, as such, could not be glossed over with the benign and patronizing attitude which was the hallmark of emancipated Jews in the West. Judaism itself was an issue. Zionism served—like the Revolution, like the secular-socialist and anti-Zionist *Bund*—a collective psychological need. It was not merely a corridor through which a higher and more successful integration into European society could be achieved.

In East Europe, the search for a new meaning or substitute to Jewish life, for new Jewish or secular values was a direct outcome of the absence of all that characterized West European Jewry: legal equality, a reformed version of Judaism, a secular culture whose benefits Jews could experience and whose values they would want to acquire. In the East, the Jews were thrown straight from the claustrophobic *shtetl* existence into the arms of either Zionism or Revolution. For young Jews, Zionism filled the gap formed by the revolt against the Orthodox father on the one hand and the disappointment with the Russian revolutionary brother, on the other. The constant, painful friction between young Zionists and the strong rabbinical establishment and the tradition they represented contrasted sharply with the distant calm with which the assimilated Jews of France, Germany, Austria-Hungary, and England regarded the religious issue. Indeed, it was this combat with traditional Judaism which gave birth in East Europe to both the budding Hebrew secular literature and those wondrous Jewish idealists who gave their life for the Revolution by which they were eventually destroyed. It also gave Zionism its special soul.

Herzl wanted to solve the plight of the Jews. But, as Ahad Ha'am phrased it, there was also the plight of Judaism, which could no longer be contained within the shackles of traditional religion and which had to find viable alternatives or disappear by attrition. Thus all the major trends which were destined to influence the State of Israel were born in Eastern Europe: socialist Zionism; religion of work; religious Zionism; the revival of Hebrew; Palestine as a spiritual center. All these, in their way, sought to give a substantive answer to a question Herzl was oblivious to. It is this phenomenon which also explains an apparent paradox in Zionist history: the western Zionists, headed by Herzl, whose Jewish background was so meager, did not find any difficulty in co-existing with the religious Zionists. In progressive western society, due respect is to be paid to faith. On the other side, the religious issue infuriated the East European Zionists who were divided between an observant minority and a rebellious secular majority.

Herzl could easily accept the religious demand that the Zionist organization desist from all "cultural work"; by definition, it would put an emphasis on secular value. But for leaders like Chaim Weizmann, a rebel against his own shtetl upbringing, the issue was of crucial importance and reason enough to break with Herzl and form, at the Second Zionist Congress, his own separate faction. For Herzl, religion had its place; the rabbis were to be respected but confined to their religious sphere, like soldiers to barracks, as is the custom of a modern progressive state. In the East, as Weizmann wrote Herzl, the rejection of religion among the youth reached such proportions that young Jews were venting their anger by desecrating Torah scrolls; in the West, such preposterous behavior could not be contemplated by those who advocated reason and tolerance.

The fact that the Jews had a religion of their own was, by itself, compatible with the Zionist wish for normalization.

After all, there were national churches in European countries, such as Greece, Rumania, Bulgaria, and Russia; there were the Anglicans and the German Lutherans; and even the universal faiths acquired in many countries a distinct national expression.

Moreover, toward the end of the nineteenth century, a tendency developed to view religion as part of that national spirit which allegedly characterizes every people. This new zeitgeist, this romantic-nationalist view, contrasted sharply with the more universal and rational approaches which prevailed in the first half of the nineteenth century and which enabled the Jews to acquire their new equality. According to this romantic view, which won many admirers in Germany, every people has its own manifest destiny and its own national "soul" and, consequently, its religion too must express these special attributes. If rational universalism was going to make way for this new brand of nationalism, the Jews could easily claim their own ancient faith as a national asset par excellence. Indeed, years before the advent of Zionism, Moses Hess, the socialist philosopher and one time collaborator or Marx and Engels, wrote that the existence of their own distinctive religion proved that the Jews were a people entitled to national independence. The existence of this both national and universal religion merely confirmed his view that the Jews were truly the first authentic nation. Thus, in western Zionists' eyes, the existence of a Jewish faith was not incongruous with the desire to be a nation like all other nations.

Max Nordau, who combined ardent Zionism with fiery atheism, brought this nationalist attitude to its extremist conclusion. Asked about the future of the Sabbath in the Jewish State, he did not exclude its optional replacement by the more universal Sunday, as is the custom of the Gentiles. Ahad Ha'am, who regarded the Jewish Sabbath as the incarnation of the Jewish spirit, was flabbergasted and infuriated by such ideas and from his Odessa home he directed at Nordau words of fury and scorn:

Not one word escaped the mouth of this Zionist sage which would testify that his heart rebels against the cancellation of the Sabbath, because of its historical and national value. The whole question, in his eyes, is purely religious and therefore he excludes himself from any direct commitment. He, the free thinker, will have his own appropriate day of rest, bereft of any religious intent, and he does not care whether the Sabbath, the Queen of Judaism, exists or not.[11]

Ahad Ha'am was convinced that East European Zionists, including free thinkers, "will feel like me as if a cold northern wind invaded their hearts and threw ice on their most sacred feelings."

There were, needless to say, other voices within Russian Zionism. In typical fashion, some of them carried the Herzlian idea to its extreme, almost fanatical, conclusion. One of these, Jacob Klatzkin, born within the Russian Pale of Settlement and later editor of *Die Welt*, the official organ of the Zionist organization, railed against the Eastern European need for "Jewish content." For Klatzkin, Zionists like Ahad Ha'am represented a galut mentality and would be responsible, if successful, for frustrating the very idea of national renaissance: "It is no accident that Zionism arose in the West and not in the East. Herzl appeared among us not from the national consciousness of a Jew but from a universal human consciousness. Not the Jew but the man in him brought him back to his people."[12]

Klatzkin claimed that the basic intention of Zionism was "to deny any conception of Jewish identity based on spiritual criteria." This is the real revolution. This is the world-destroying and world-building movement which is diametrically opposed to the East European attitude. That attitude, having "none of the heroism of revelation," viewed Zionism as a continuation of Jewish history and "draws its energies directly from the sources of Judaism."

Klatzkin represented an extremist view, both in the way he depicted the clash between East and West and in his denial of any element of continuation between Jewish existence and the future society of new Jews. Ahad Ha'am, too, represented only a faction of Eastern Zionists, among whom there were many ardent followers of the Herzlian view. But the clash between these two dogmatic personalities expressed the emotional upheaval sweeping the Jewish world east of Vienna. It was that world which fed the future state of Israel with pioneers, settlers, and leaders. From them, its East European founders, Israel inherited its habit of continuous soul-searching concerning its identity as successor to that ancient Jewish tradition on which so many of her founders were raised and against which so many rebelled. All the problems which lie heavily on Israel's soul politic—the Jewish nature of Israel, its relations with the Diaspora and the outside world, its attachment to the Jewish heritage—are the offspring of that intellectual ferment which characterized East European Zionism in its early heyday. The search for new values, for a contemporary gospel expressing the change in Jewish society, which would renew, or even replace, the old, crumbling, irreparable Jewish civilization of yesteryear, did not come from the salons of western Jewry but from those for whom Zionism was the direct result of their revolt against both the father's home and the rabbi's synagogue.

2

THE MEANING OF
NORMALIZATION

IN spite of all the differences within Zionism about the content of Jewish nationalism, one theme united the warring factions: the need to create a new breed of Jews in the new society destined to be established in Palestine. "Our revolution," wrote A. D. Gordon, that secular prophet of the return to the soil and the religion of work, "is the revolution of the man in the Jew."[1] That revolution has a universal human value, and through it the highest ideals of mankind will merge into a new Jewish existence.

This metamorphosis of the Jewish person will remove the defects formed by the long galut. Through this revolution, Israel will return not only to its land but also to the family of nations. Again, looking back at the strife-strewn history of Zionism, one is impressed by the consensus supporting this idea of the return of the Jews to their rightful place as human beings and as equal partners among the Gentiles of the earth. The galut is darkness, and redemption lies in this twofold revolution of the individual and of the people. Because of this craving for a return to normalcy, the great bulk of Orthodox Judaism resisted Zionism and proclaimed its message to be a heresy, a contradiction of the very tenets of Judaism. Zionism sought to transform the status of Jews among the nations—from a persecuted minority awaiting the coming of the Messiah to equal partners in a secular world.

It required a major mental readjustment. The Jewish people,

the chosen people, the people of the binding Covenant with
God, who gave the world its messianic vision, according to
Zionist philosophy, would have to re-examine these very foundation stones. The idea of a national revival for the Jews drew
its initial inspiration from the successful growth of modern
national liberation movements, such as the Bulgarian, the Ru-
manian, and the Italian, in the second half of the nineteenth
century. But these national movements were bereft of any
messianic message and did not pretend to speak in the name of
an exclusiveness with universal and cosmic significance. Arthur Hertzberg put this dilemma in the following words:

Religious messianism had always imagined the Redemption as a confrontation between the Jew and God. The Gentile played a variety of
roles in this drama—as chastising rod in the divine hand, as the enemy to be discomfited, or, at very least, as the spectator to pay homage
at the end of the play—but none of these parts are indispensable to the
plot. In the cutting edge of Zionism, in its most revolutionary expression, the essential dialogue is now between the Jew and the nations of
the earth. What marks modern Zionism as a fresh beginning in Jewish
history is that its ultimate values derive from the general milieu. The
Messiah is now identified with the dream of an age of individual
liberty, national freedom, and economic and social justice—i.e., with
the progressive faith of the nineteenth century.[2]

Indeed, the change brought about by Zionism was so radical, so
revisionist, that some of its implications were never expressed
directly.

The first implication was a revised attitude toward anti-
Semitism. Hatred of the Jews—not to mention violence against
them—was, of course, regarded by all Zionists as a manifestation of evil. But if the inferiority and the abnormal status of the
galut Jew explained, at least partially, the animosity toward
him, this antagonism could now be seen in a new light. Because
the Zionists were determined to take their fate into their own
hands and remove from a theological context their relations
with the outside world, there arose a need to explain this ani-

mosity in new, rational terms. As long as galut was explainable in terms of divine punishment, reasoning about it was unnecessary. But with Zionism, galut was regarded neither as punishment nor manifest destiny but rather as a humiliating disease to be cured. Anti-Semitism was, therefore, a force not only to be reckoned with but also, to some degree, to be understood and diagnosed with a view to finding a solution: The rational response was a political remedy which would resolve the conflict between a "sick" minority and a "healthy" majority.

Indeed, Herzl's treatment of anti-Semitism in his *Die Judenstaat* was so unemotional—and occasionally even patronizing—that in a post-Auschwitz world it is difficult to digest. Herzl analyzed the inevitable clash and saw Zionism as bringing relief to both Jew and Gentile. It would also solve the problem of Jews who decided to remain behind, facilitating their complete assimilation and absorption into Christian society. Zionism removed the malignant tumor, and that tumor lay not in any personal fault but in the reality of Gentiles pitted against Jews: In anti-Semitism he saw the elements of "cruel sport, of common commercial rivalry, of inherited prejudice, of religious intolerance—but also a supposed need for self-defense."[3]

Herzl demonstrated a largesse toward anti-Semites. He planned to include "decent anti-Semites" to assist in the Zionist undertaking, "while respecting their integrity—which is important to us."

Herzl also set a precedent for future Zionist leaders by dealing with Wenzel von Plehve, the anti-Semitic czarist minister of the interior. Because Zionism sought to return the Jews as equal partners to the world scene, it would speak as equal to equal even to those whose hatred of the galut Jews was their second nature. In a similar vein, Jabotinsky, leader of the Revisionist Right, described the "objective nature" of anti-Semitism. In his testimony before the Palestine Royal Commission in 1937—after the rise of Nazism in Germany—he declared: "The cause of our suffering is the very fact of the Diaspora. It is not the anti-Semitism of men; it is, above all, the anti-Semitism of things, the inherent xenophobia of the body social or the body economic under which we suffer."[4]

The systematic murder of six million European Jews put an end to such cool and objective indifference to anti-Semitism and anti-Semites. After the Holocaust, it became impossible to resort to Herzl's phrase about "decent anti-Semites." Nevertheless, the strength of the Zionist sentiment is so great that in spite of the Holocaust it continues to guide Israel's policy. In the 1950s and 1960s, many Israelis regarded as natural the new links formed between the Jewish state and those European circles whose salons are rank with the age-old anti-Semitism. In the first years of Israel's existence, one could occasionally detect a sort of latent pride: The Zionist dream became a reality because the ex-persecuted were such respectable masters that their ex-persecutors sought their company. In those years, one could have found many other similar manifestations. The new Jew, the proud Israeli, was ready to associate with his recently found equal rather than with his "miserable step-brother," the galut Jew. And when *Time* magazine, in its first cover story on the young state, in August 16, 1948, wrote that the young Israelis "run to the big-boned, blue-eyed, blond athlete type associated with anti-Semitic persecutions," this was regarded as one more proof that Herzl's "wondrous breed of new Maccabees" had indeed sprung forth.

The second implication arising out of the return of the Jews to the international community related to a critical re-examination of traditional Jewish civilization. If galut was no more a preordained divine infliction and if its very essence was to be negated, then Zionism had to re-evaluate Jewish history itself. Consequently, it was permissible not only to break away from the Pale of Settlement mentality and to bring down the walls of the rabbinical establishment but also to question everything which was sacred and hallowed in Jewish tradition.

Thus within Zionism there grew a non-Jewish, even anti-

Jewish sentiment, stunning in its strength and in its longings for the pagan and the Gentile. True, this sentiment preceded Zionism, and the rebellion against traditional Judaism nourished both the Haskalah (Enlightenment) literature and the turn toward socialist and revolutionary activity among young Jews in Eastern Europe. Zionism did not give birth to this moood—to a certain extent it was assisted by it—but it also gave it a legitimate national justification which no socialist revolution could offer. Because of Zionism, an author could write in Hebrew, and with a strong sense of nationalist pride, tracts castigating Judaism for real and imaginary faults and yet retain his standing as a Jew within the community. It was permissible to cast stones at everything sacred in father's home and to admire that which was anathema to Jews throughout the ages. *Facing the Statue of Apollo*, written in 1899 by Saul Tschernichovsky, one of the greatest Hebrew poets, is a well-known example of this new defiance. The poet describes himself facing the pagan god—"the youth-god, sublime and free, the acme of beauty!" He refers to the eternal war between the pagan god and the Jews and proclaims: "I am the first of my race to return to you." He turns away from the old God and yields to the forces of "life and courage and beauty," mourning the wild god who had "stormed Canaan in conquest" only to be "tied up with the straps phylacteries."[5]

It became permissible to advocate mixed marriages, as Lilienblum and Klatzkin had done. It was even permissible to re-examine the traditional attitude toward Christianity and to Jesus Christ. Joseph Chaim Brenner, a famous socialist Hebrew author and playwright who was assassinated by Arabs in 1921, created a minor scandal when he wrote:

As for myself, the Old Testament does not have that value which everybody shouts about: the Book of Books, the eternal book, the Holy Scriptures. From the hypnotism of the twenty-four books of the Bible, I have long freed myself. Many profane books, written in later periods, are closer to me and greater in my eyes; but the same importance which I find and recognize in the Bible, as remnants of ancient memo-

ries, as the embodiment of the spirit of our people and of our humanity throughout so many generations—this same importance I also find
in the books of the New Testament. The New Testament too is a bone
of our bones and a flesh of our flesh.[6]

Even the Christian theory ascribing deity to Jesus did not deter
Brenner. He failed to see any danger in it: "a person of Israel
can be a good Jew, devoted to his people, despite the fact that
he . . . regards the son of our people—the poor Jew, Jesus of
Nazareth—with religious piety."

Such voices, though emanating from central figures within
the Zionist movement, did not represent the mainstream point
of view, and Brenner's dictum on the New Testament and
Christ, which was merely one aspect of his frontal attack on the
Jewish religion, caused a furor both inside and outside Palestine.
However, that such voices did exist and that they were a legitimate aspect of the Zionist reassessment of Jewish past is relevant. In fact, these anti-Jewish moods were reinforced by the
new reality of the *Yishuv*, the Jewish community in Palestine.

In the special atmosphere of the Yishuv, the discrepancy
between past and present, between old and new Jews, seemed
palpable and irrefutable. A succinct statement of this growing
sense of alienation from the past is found in "The Sermon," a
famous short story, written by Haim Hazaz, one of Israel's
more illustrious writers, after the outbreak of World War II,
when the Jews were already subject to Nazi terror. The hero of
the story examines the nature of Judaism and Zionism and
finally reaches the verdict, pronounced in short, cutting sen-
tences: "Zionism and Judaism are not at all the same, but two
things quite different from each other, and maybe even two
things directly opposite to each other! At any rate far from the
same. When a man can no longer be a Jew, he becomes a
Zionist."[7]

The third implication was connected with Hazaz's verdict
and concerns the relationship between the New Jews of the
Yishuv and their "miserable step-brothers" in the Diaspora.

The settlement of Palestine by a growing number of Jews enhanced two basic streams which flowed out of the spring of Zionist ideology: a further alienation from Jewish past and a further opening toward the outside world. In Palestine, in Eretz Israel, a new community of Jews was formed. From the beginning, this community avoided using the term "Jew." It was a Hebrew Yishuv; all of its institutions followed suit: the Histadrut was the trade union federation of the Hebrew workers; so were the associations of doctors, lawyers, writers, and journalists; all were Hebrew, not Jewish. Tel Aviv was hallowed not as the first Jewish but as the first Hebrew city. A common slogan read: "Hebrew, speak Hebrew." Yiddish was despised and often ostracized. Like the Reformed communities in America—who similarly adopted the term "Hebrew"—and the assimilated French Jews—who opted for "Israelite"—the new Jews were eager to shake off the word "Jew" as a means of signifying the change taking place in their lives. But unlike French and American Jews, "Hebrew" represented the will to create a new people, a new nation, a new goy, who live in their own land and speak their own language. The Palestinian young Hebrew was the super Jew, and the rise of the Sabra cult accentuated this divergence between new and old.

In Palestine there existed a small community of Orthodox Jews, the "Old Yishuv" as it came to be known before the Zionists arrived. But from the days of the Second Aliyah, the wave of socialist pioneers who came to Palestine from pogrom-ridden Russia after 1905, the Yishuv was dominated by a strong secular element. The former rebels against father and rabbi became leaders of that Yishuv, and they led the way toward Zionist self-fulfillment. All the paraphernalia of the hated galut—Yiddish, the shtetl, the peddler trades—disappeared and in their stead appeared the characteristics of the new Jew: Hebrew, communal settlements, manual work, a return to the soil, attachment to nature, a newly acquired rootedness. The new Sabra character was, finally, a Jewish peasant, a goyish type, characterized by a healthy earthiness. He could be

THE MEANING OF NORMALIZATION

recognized and identified, just as Jabotinsky, in his Herzl obituary, wished. Yet, it is interesting to note that, despite this growing divergence, the Hebrew Yishuv moved toward less fricton with traditional rabbinical Judaism. There were, of course, political divisions and hotly debated disputes: on the rights of women, on freedom of conscience, on the meaning of Judaism. But the explosive tension which marked the East European experience was gone. The old Orthodox Yishuv was marginal and lacked political power. The hegemony belonged, within a short time, to the socialist Labor movement. Father's home became remote and from an object of rebellion it was transformed into a subject of homesickness. The exodus of the sons from the shtetl diluted much of the former bitterness.

Jewishness thus meant mainly to be a Hebrew, to love the land, to be attached to nature, to give tradition a new national and social meaning. Absalom Feinberg symbolized this new mood. One of the first Sabras, destined to die in World War I while serving the pro-British Nili spying group, he interrupted a play depicting the persecution of the Jews. "Not in Eretz Israel!" he shouted: "When we shall have beautiful olive orchards, the lifework of generations, then the people growing up in their shades will be ready to die in order to protect the trees."[8] This was the essence of the new Jews.

The lessening friction was also explicable in terms of the new reality. The nucleus of the novel society was concentrated in communal settlements far removed—physically as well as psychologically—from the religious groups. Distance breeds tolerance, and the harangues against religion were limited to writers like Brenner, who continued to castigate the galut mentality, as well as to work against any attempt to introduce religion into Palestine.

In the communal settlements, Jewish tradition gave birth to a new interpretation. The Sabbath became a day of rest, to be dispensed with whenever necessary. Marriage ceremonies were not always celebrated, and when they were, this became a mere appendage to cohabitation, a favor to faraway parents or a half-hearted attempt to prevent a total break with the past. Occasionally, some settlements went to fanatic extremes: anything but the natural, healthy, and earthy was frowned upon. The poet Abraham Shlonsky described the derogatory reaction from his kibbutz comrades when they discovered that he was writing for a literary magazine—a typically cultural Jewish activity to be avoided in the new land.

The Jewish holidays acquired a new social, agricultural, or national meaning. In the Seder ceremony, the traditional Haggadah was replaced by modern writings and poems; Shavuot, the Pentecost, or Festival of Weeks, which signified the giving of the Torah at Sinai, was celebrated only in its earthly, agricultural aspect: The first fruit of the season was presented in a ceremony seeking to recreate biblical scenes. Chanukah became the celebration of Maccabean heroism and Jewish liberation from a foreign yoke—and, occasionally, even signifying a class struggle— Rosh Hashanah was simply the New Year and an opportune time for self-reckoning. New holidays were invented: a new year for the trees; a celebration of Bar Kochba's last revolt against the Romans; Herzl's birthday; and, of course, the first of May, the international day of workers' solidarity.

There were some difficulties: What could one do about Yom Kippur, whose purely religious significance was too obvious to be tampered with? The different settlements, obviously belonging to different political movements, failed to produce a uniform response. Some, like A. D. Gordon, saw in it a day in which the individual loses his self and becomes a part of a unified whole, a limb in the body of the community, a member of a higher personality. But such theories never became part of the Zionist socialist dogma. Among the new pioneers and settlers, many—perhaps the majority—did not observe Yom Kippur and some workers' restaurants were actually open on its holy eve; others were allowed to revert to the old ways and, out of instinct or respect for tradition, justified their "deviation." Hannah Senesh, a poet and a member of a kibbutz, who was executed after parachuting into Nazi Hungary in an attempt to organize its Jews, wrote in her diary on the eve of Yom Kippur 1941:

I'm not fasting, because I don't feel the need. In my opinion, the only value of fasting is for the Jews in the Diaspora to express their solidarity. I feel I have other ways of expressing my ties with Judaism, and I'll forgo this one, which is completely alien to me.[9]

This divergence between the devout tradition and the new secular interpretation, between old and new Jews, is best demonstrated by one instance: In 1914, a mission of Orthodox rabbis, headed by the pro-Zionist Rabbi Kook, set out from its enclosed Jerusalem quarters to visit the new communal settlements in the north of the country, to learn how serious were the breaches against religion and to attempt to bring back the errants to some measure of Jewishness. The odd encounter brought together two separate worlds which only a generation before shared the same tradition.

What the rabbis found, to their distress, was a tragic relinquishing of any semblance of religion. Their report was a litany of woes: in Hadera, "the religious situation among the workers is wild . . . they baked bread on Passover"; in Zichron Yaacov, "the teachers do their best to uproot religion from the hearts of their pupils"; in Merhavia, "there is no kosher kitchen and on Yom Kippur only fifteen out of fifty observed the fast"; in Poriah, "the young break the Sabbath and eat non-kosher food"; in Kinneret, "there is neither prayer nor fasting on Yom Kippur; bread is eaten on Passover and there is no trace of religion."[10]

There were, naturally, some rebels against this drastic transition. Reading through the Second Aliyah literature (and how abundantly these few thousand did write!) one comes across a longing for the old world ostensibly shattered beyond repair. In one of the ever-debating workers' assemblies, where Yiddish was proscribed and despised, one member who wanted to speak his mother's tongue, broke down:

What do you want of me? I have accepted with love all the torments of this land; I broke my back in hard manual labor while starving for food; I fulfill the tenet of Hebrew self-work with devotion and dedication; I am malaria stricken. Is all this nothing in your eyes that you wish to deprive me of the language on which I grew up and to which I am attached with all my heart? Do you also want to make me dumb in this land?[11]

And occasionally a member of a kibbutz wandered into a traditional home; his heart was filled with joy and nostalgia at the reminders of the old ways: the family seated at the dinner table, the candles, the service, the challah.

But these were mere deviations from the main route which led away from galut and religion toward a brave new future. Under the sun of Canaan, in the fields of Jezreel and on the hills of Judea, the galut seemed even more despicable, even more inferior and its negation became a common slogan, a solid foundation on which the Yishuv mentality was based. Ben Gurion laid down the rules regarding the future attitude of Labor Zionism to the Diaspora and what it represented:

A new yardstick will be applied to our old satchel. Anything which is great and important enough for our present road, we shall carry with us; anything which is small, rotten, and smacks of galut we shall throw away so that it will disappear with the bad heritage of the dead past, so that this past will not cast its shadow over our new soul and will not desecrate the sanctity of our redemption.

And when Ben Gurion talked about the new Hebrew worker, the former Jew who perhaps had landed in Jaffa only a short time before, he exclaimed:

The worker of Eretz Israel differs from the Jewish worker in Galut in his historical origin [sic], his economic attitude, his social goals, his national destiny. . . . Not a new branch grafted to an old tradition is he; a new tree of a workers' class has grown to the Jewish people out of their new land.[12]

Anyone reading these lines—taken from a legion of similar utterances—realizes that they consciously sought to bypass large portions of Jewish history. Here was a collision between two different concepts of what "redemption" means. On the one side, stood secular Zionists from Left and Right—Jabotinsky as well as Ben Gurion—who denied the validity and relevance of Jewish history from the last revolt against the Romans to the Return to Zion. On the other side, stood the traditional Jewish outlook which belittled the Jewish rebellions against the Romans and put its emphasis on the great works of scholarship created in galut. The secular view went so far as to downgrade even the Talmud and the "oral Torah," the guide by which Jews lived and which embodied their own unique legal system. Constant attempts were made to exclude its study from the Yishuv schools' curricula.

According to the secular outlook, Zionism equaled redemption because it returned the Jewish people to their rightful place in history as an independent nation; according to the religious non-Zionist outlook, redemption remained a religious messianic concept and Zionism, by replacing it with a secular political concept, transgressed against the divine purpose of Jewish existence.

With the growth of the Hebrew Yishuv, the emphasis on the secular concept of redemption—secular messianism, as it was often referred to by Labor Zionists—became more pronounced. Zionism was the salvation and salvation meant a new brand of Jews.

During the 1940s and 1950s, this process yielded a strange fruit: the movement of young Hebrews, or Canaanites, became audible and active and took normalization to its extremist conclusion. Headed by Yonathan Ratosh, a gifted and innovative poet, this group sought to cut the ties uniting the Yishuv with its Jewish origins. The group was always small and lacked political organization, but its influence belied its size. It was formed in the forties, reached its zenith in the early fifties, and included some of the brightest young intellectuals in the country. Its influence was described by Baruch Kurzweil, famous literary critic and a professor at Bar Ilan University, as having created a major Israeli school of Hebrew literature.

The Canaanites' theory was confused and their reasoning muddled. They regarded Palestine and its inhabitants as one organic unity, a new Hebrew people which had to be strengthened by the imposition of Hebrew culture, intermarriage and, above all, by severing Zionist ties with Jews and the Jewish heritage. Judaism was a corruption of the pure original Hebrew spirit and, therefore, had to be eradicated. In the words of Yonathan Ratosh, the founder of the movement:

Judaism, all of it, its values, the sum total of its history, is foreign to this generation of the native-born, to its young men and boys. . . . It is foreign to them because the social experience out of which and into which they grow is, by its very nature, the opposite of the Jewish experience.[13]

The appeal of the Canaanites' views to the younger generation was clear. They expressed, in strong words, moods and sentiments shared by many. Indeed, they carried Zionist doctrine to a seemingly logical end. The whole aim of the Return to Zion was to rectify the abnormality inherent in Jewish existence. It sought to solve the Jewish question by achieving normalization through creating a nation-state like all other nations. Today, some of the Canaanite utterances sound positively anti-Semitic. Again, Ratosh in his Canaanite Manifesto:

There is no Hebrew unless he is a Hebrew, son of this land of the Hebrews, and everyone else is excluded. Anyone coming from the Jewish Diaspora is a Jew and not a Hebrew and cannot be anything but a Jew—bad or good, proud or cowardly, he is still a Jew. The Jew and the Hebrew cannot be identical and he who is a Jew cannot become a Hebrew.[14]

To replace the word "Hebrew" by "German" or "French" is to appreciate the extent of the anti-Jewish sentiment pervading the Canaanite outlook. The Canaanites were extremist and marginal, but many of their fellow-travellers regarded the Zionist process as having been terminated: the Hebrew child was ready to leave his parental Jewish home. The Canaanites' rejection of the traditional Jew, their infatuation with the native-born and the native land was in accord with current moods. There has always been a narcissistic streak in the Sabra mentality; the Canaanites appealed to the vanity which characterized the native Israeli. They reviled the ghetto Jew by contrasting him with the Sabra:

The main difference nowadays is not between the various Jewish communities overseas but between all these communities on the one hand, and the fast-growing Hebrew younger generation manifesting itself in the Sabra type—the native-born, who is notably un-Jewish in his physique, outlook, and way of life.[15]

It is ironic that this was written while the Jews of Europe were being slaughtered or their remnants seeking refuge in Palestine.

The Canaanites were blind to reality—to Arab enmity, to Jewish roots—and they brought the Zionist idea of normalization ad absurdum. But like all such absurd conclusions, it contained a grain of relevance. If the Jews were to be normal, they should be subject to rules which govern other immigrant, formative societies.

At the center and in the mainstream of the Yishuv, however, Zionist dogma was being reinforced by acts and deeds: the Balfour Declaration and the League of Nations' Mandate fulfilled the Herzlian vision of recognition by, and support of, the international community for Jewish national renewal. In Palestine a truly unique society of new Jews emerged, as removed from their galut parents as the Zionist writers and thinkers could wish. The Jews indeed were becoming a goy—a nation; the Jew was indeed becoming a non-Jewish goy, a semi-Gentile. So forceful was this mood that it survived even the ongoing war with the Arabs, Britain's betrayal of the Jews, and the horrors of Auschwitz—events which had a shocking impact on Zionist history. From this idea of normalization came a change in the attitude toward anti-Semitism, the alienation from the Jewish past, and the growth of a new Hebrew culture and society.

Behind all these developments loomed a larger issue—the ever unsolved question which dominated Zionist thought: Will the new Hebrew nation, on regaining sovereignty in its land, forsake all claims to Jewish exclusivist tradition and become a nation like every other nation? Will this process remove the foundation stone upon which the house of Jewish thought was built? Will the new Jews differ from other peoples only as the French differ from the English, or will they retain some universal message, some uniqueness, some "otherness"—the heirlooms of their past—in the world they seek to join? If they were going to be a goy, what would happen to that special heritage which distinguished between them and the rest of the world? If Zionism was to demolish all these past tenets bequeathed to it by Judaism, what would remain of Jewish destiny? "How," asked the atheist writer Brenner, "shall we be us without us?"

3

RELIGIOUS VERSUS SECULAR
TENSIONS

For generations—in fact, since they became a people—
Jews saw themselves as different and separate from the "Gentiles of the earth." The Covenant between God and His people
and the receiving of the Torah at Mount Sinai lay at the heart
of Jewish thought, Jewish Law, and Jewish existence. This eternal Covenant lends to Jewish existence, from a religious point
of view, its special status among the nations. The words of
Exodus speak clearly: "If ye will hearken unto My voice indeed, and keep My covenant, then ye shall be Mine own treasure [am segula] from among all peoples" (19:5). The Covenant
clothes Jews with that very sanctity which separates them
from the other peoples. Chosenness depends on abiding by the
Covenant and on the observance of the Law. Chosenness is
that state which follows the prophecy "and ye shall be unto me
a kingdom of priests and a holy nation." Isaiah's comforting
prophecy relates Israel's universal destiny with the Covenant:
"I will give these for a Covenant of the people, for a light of the
nations." The severance of the Jews from the other nations, as
well as their millennial role, are all attributable to the Covenant: "Ye shall be holy unto me, for I the Lord am holy and
have severed you from other peoples that ye should be mine."

These well-known passages explain why it is impossible,
from the traditional viewpoint, to separate the idea of chosenness, of a "treasure nation" [am segula], from the concept of
the Covenant and the observance of Jewish religious law and

how false it is to relate these religious paradigms to secular values. It is futile to transplant the biblical injunctions into a secular context and support this by referring to the prophets' universal visions of social justice and peace among nations. The belief in one God and the revelation on Mount Sinai alone endowed the people of Israel with their special status among the nations.

Thus, it was unavoidable that the growth of a new secular Judaism, in a post-French Revolution world, would crack the old foundations. When faith began to disappear and the actual laws were disobeyed, the raison d'être for Jewish chosenness—which had its justification only within the confines of religion—eroded together with the decline of Jewish civilization. Furthermore, not only Judaism was being transformed by the new era. The world in which Jews lived was undergoing radical changes and was totally different from the one in which Jewish exclusiveness developed. The pagan world, against which Judaism's monotheism shone brightly, was gone; the new civilization, based in part on Jewish moral concepts, combined advanced Christian monotheism with the French Revolution ideas of equality. Such changes affected even Orthodox canon law. Within its narrow confines, rabbis and sages began to make a distinction between the ancient pagans—against whom the religious injunctions fully prevailed—and the Christians, who were recognized, because of their monotheism, as a special category.

If rigid Orthodox law could adapt its interpretations to the modern progressive era, how much more so the young secular, assimilated or reformed Jews. After all, modern Jews in Western Europe responded to emancipation by renouncing any national extra-religious claim and by delegating Judaism to the private domain. Moses Hess explained in 1862—some thirty-five years before the advent of Herzlian Zionism—that "until the French Revolution, the Jewish people were the only people in the world whose religion was at once nationalist and universalist. . . . Since the French Revolution, the French, as well as other people who followed them, have become our noble rivals and faithful allies."[1] To the reformed communities in the West, as well as the young revolutionaries in the East, chosenness, in the religious Jewish sense, had lost its meaning by the time Zionism made its appearance. The spirit of ecumenical tolerance and the waves of the future socialist revolution swept aside the old concept. In the new, progressive world about to awaken, the Covenant seemed an ancient irrelevance to the growing numbers of modern Jews. In fact, toward the end of the nineteenth century, the enlightened Jews were the vanguard of universal equality and ecumenical fraternity, while in major European countries new doctrines of racial superiority, of gentile "chosenness," took root: pan-Germanism in Germany and among German-speaking minorities; pan-Slavism in czarist Russia; French integral nationalism in the country which formulated the universal rules of equality. Chosenness, toward the end of the century, was certainly not solely a Jewish concern.

For the Zionists—especially for those who lived in Eastern Europe—the question could not be shoved aside that easily. Zionism rehabilitated the Jews not as individuals but as a collective body. What would become of the old foundations? In this new reality, how could the idea of chosenness, of the "treasure nation," find its place? Indeed, could it find a place at all? This question could not be dismissed by resorting to Ben Gurion's avoidance of Jewish history in exile, by eliminating the Talmud, and hallowing the Bible. The Book of Books— from Genesis through the Prophets to Psalms—sings the glories of the Covenant between God and his people, praises their special mission, and bewails the transgressions against the Covenant and the Law.

Secular Zionists had some inherent difficulty in delineating the place religion would occupy in the new Jewish nationalism. Despite the analogies with other national churches, Judaism is essentially different. It is a total entity covering all aspects of individual, collective, and national rules of conduct. It does not recognize any distinction between secular and religious law. It unites the people of Israel with the religion of Israel and the land of Israel. An attempt to rid Zionism of all religious underpinnings would immediately result in a set of paradoxes. What is the Sabbath? A purely religious asset which can be dispensed with or part of a national bequest to be retained? Is circumcision—a rite to which some modern Jews objected very strongly—an act symbolizing the entrance into a nation or merely the religious act signifying the acceptance of Abraham's Covenant with the Lord? And the Promised Land itself—the beloved Zion whose very name was the movement itself: Was not the Jewish claim to it based on Divine promise which was at the core of the very religion being discarded? Alternatively, was not the claim to Eretz Israel as an independent national right based on Jewish history? Herzl and his western friends, ignorant as they were of things Jewish, were soon to appreciate the complexity involved in eliciting a national identity out of a religion-dominated civilization. When Zionists who were not recognized as Jews by Jewish religious law sought to join the Zionist movement, the question of who was a Jew (destined to plague the Jewish state with bitter controversies) reared its unpleasant head. If the Jews were going to be a nation like all nations, why should religion be the doorkeeper? Under Jewish religious law, Jewishness is governed by the concept of the Covenant. A Jew either is born into it—by being born to a Jewish mother—or accepts the Covenant through conversion. But how could such rules apply to a secular, normal nation? Did it make any sense that a movement which spoke in the name of national liberation should insist on religious rites as credentials for joining it? Yet any deviation from religious rules automatically introduced an incorrigible split between religious and nonreligious Zionists. Consequently, Herzl, whose son was never circumcised, ruled against a secular definition of "Who is a Jew"— a decision destined to be quoted with affirmation seventy years later by Israel's supreme court.

To explain this and similar paradoxes, secular Zionists resorted to Ahad Ha'am's interpretation of Jewish history. Ahad Ha'am resisted all temptation to turn the Jews into merely "another nation," nor did he seek, like Herzl and his followers, to be integrated into modern progressive society. His confidence and trust in modernity were shaped by what he saw around him: a growing enmity toward all Jews by both the Russian intelligentsia and the new revolutionaries. For Ahad Ha'am, secularist that he was, Jewish tradition itself was imperiled, and it was the task of Zionism to come to its rescue. That tradition, the totality of Jewish history, had religious manifestations, but these were merely one aspect, one form, one expression of the Jewish national spirit. The religious aspect became naturally dominant in exile, where, in order to keep the unity of the nation, it gradually replaced other facets of the inherent national spirit. Jewish culture was forced, as it were, into such sublimation by external circumstance. It was this view of Jewish nationalism which enabled Zionists to incorporate major attributes of Jewish tradition and religion.

Ahad Ha'am's views were not shared by "political Zionists" who had no patience with the emphasis he put on spirituality and his alleged lack of sensitivity to the dire needs of suffering Jews. But there was a far wider consensus on his view of the role of religion in Jewish nationalism. Thus Ahad Ha'am's attitude to the Bible, which lent the Book of Books a meaning transcending religion, defined its place in Zionist—and later, Israeli—thought:

Even the nonbeliever, if he is a national Jew, cannot regard the Holy Scriptures solely from a literary point of view, but he combines a literary and a national point of view. . . . He senses an innermost feeling which attaches him to the Bible, a feeling of special intimacy tinged by sanctity, in that a thousand invisible arteries go out from him and spawn generation after generation reaching into the depths of distant past.[2]

Hence the crossroads at which Zionism found itself from its early days:

Will the sons of Israel live in their state according to their own unique spirit and give life and develop their own national assets which were bequeathed to their past, or will their state merely be another European colony in Asia, a colony which looks up to the metropolis, seeking to imitate her in every way?[3]

This view was responsible for ensuring the survival of the Zionist movement, not as a sectarian group seeking autonomy for Jews but as a widely based national movement which could unite religious and secular elements and draw on current ideas of national liberation, as well as on the main features of Jewish tradition to be "translated" into secular and national concepts.

Thus, the claim to Eretz Israel could be established without invoking God's promise to His children and without tying the concept of a modern redemption to the messianic vision. These religious expressions are but one facet of the Jewish spirit which, after the exile of the Jews from their land, naturally took precedence. This view enabled Zionists to invoke the Bible as the land-title over Eretz Israel—as Ben Gurion often did—without observing religious laws and without accepting its beliefs.

At the other end of the spectrum, among religious Zionists, a converse process took place. Peace with the heretic and nonobservant Zionists could be facilitated because of the totality of Jewish religion, which regards the Return to the Holy Land and its settlement as a most exalted religious commandment. Coexisting with secular Zionists was possible because the secular law-breakers were also the legitimate bearers of these commandments and were carrying out one of Judaism's cherished faiths—the Ingathering of the Exiles. Some religious sages went further: It was even permissible to see in the Return to Zion the beginning of Redemption in its traditional, religious meaning as ushering in a messianic period. In other words, just as the secular view saw in religion a valid expression of the national spirit, so did the religious view recognize Jewish nationalism as valid expression of the religious spirit.

Of all religious personalities, the Yishuv's chief rabbi, Abraham Isaac Kook (1865–1935), symbolizes this compromise between the two parts of the Zionist movement. Rabbi Kook, posthumously destined to be claimed as the guiding light of Gush Emunim, invoked the unity of nationality and religion in order to justify this cooperation:

It is a grave error to be insensitive to the distinctive unity of the Jewish spirit, to imagine that the Divine nature which uniquely characterizes Israel is comparable to the spiritual content of all the other national civilizations. This error is the source of the attempt to sever the national from the religious element of Judaism. Such a division would falsify both our nationalism and our religion, for every element of thought, emotion, and idealism that is present in the Jewish people belongs to an indivisible entity, and all together make up its specific character.[4]

Against this background of a common link between secular and religious Zionists, based on the versatility of Jewish experience, should be seen the Zionist attempt to wrestle with the issue of traditional Jewish exclusiveness. The issue itself did not trouble the great majority of political Zionists involved as they were with the practical hardships of turning a dream into reality. The principal goal was to save the Jews from their misery and to establish a base of Palestine. Naturally, the Jews would establish a perfect, exemplary society which would lead the other nations by showing the right way to progressive modernity. But that striving toward a good and just society could not pretend to be a substitute to Jewish chosenness: the declared aim of every national liberation involves such utopian proclamations. To the Zionists, what mattered was that Israel become a nation of healthy, liberated people.

There were rebels against this thesis not only outside the Zionist camp, among the great majority of Orthodox Jews, but also within it. Judah Leon Magnes, American reform rabbi, founder and first president of the Hebrew University, became famous in the thirties for his opposition to a national Jewish state in Palestine. In a pamphlet entitled "Like All the Nations?" published in 1929 in the midst of Arab riots against Jews, Magnes dared attack the very premise of Zionist dogma by comparing it with the traditional Jewish vocation:

> The desire for power and conquest seems to be normal to many human beings and groups, and we, being the ruled everywhere, must rule; being the minority everywhere, we must here be in a majority. . . . We are to have a Fatherland, and we are to encourage feelings of pride, honor, glory that are part of the paraphernalia of the ordinary nationalistic patriotism. In the face of such dangers, one thinks of the dignity and originality of that passage of the liturgy which praises the Lord of all things that our portion is not theirs and our lot not like that of the multitude.[5]

And this view was seconded by Martin Buber, who said, in the midst of World War II:

> I am setting up Hebrew humanism in opposition to that Jewish nationalism which regards Israel as a nation like unto other nations and recognizes no task for Israel save that of preserving and asserting itself. But no nation in the world has this as its only task, for just as an individual who wishes merely to preserve and assert himself leads an unjustified and meaningless existence, so a nation with no other aim deserves to pass away.
>
> By opposing Hebrew humanism to a nationalism which is nothing but empty self-assertion, I wish to indicate that, at this juncture, the Zionist movement must decide either for national egoism or national humanism. If it decides in favor of national egoism, it too will suffer the fate which will soon befall all shallow nationalism, i.e., nationalism which does not set the nation a true supernational task. If it decides in favor of Hebrew humanism, it will be strong and effective long after shallow nationalism has lost all meaning and justification, for it will have something to say and to bring to mankind.
>
> Israel is not a nation like other nations, no matter how much its representatives have wished it during certain eras.[6]

Magnes and Buber did not succeed in changing the course of Zionism, and the Holocaust and Israel's emergence finally relegated their views of an extra-nationalist Zionism into oblivion.

To the contrary, Zionist thinking was more influenced by the other end of the spectrum—by those who wanted to eradicate any relic of past Jewish uniqueness. A blunt spokesman for this view was Brenner, whose angry homilies against retaining the past became the hallmark of the radical labor view. In Brenner's writings, the "negation of galut" is equated with the negation of Jewish history and is coupled with angry warnings against its continuation in the Jewish homeland. Brenner refused to admire Jewish survival per se, because "existence itself does not attest to its importance." He denigrated the cherished values of Judaism. To be the "treasure nation," according to Brenner, is to turn tradition upside down: "We exist. We live. Yes. But what is our life? We have no inheritance, and what we have inherited—the rabbinical literature—we would have been better off without."

Hence, the only solution was total, unmitigated normalization: "If we do not become now, with the changing circumstances of our environment, the 'treasure nation'—i.e. a nation like all other nations, who are all a treasure unto themselves—we shall be lost as a nation."[7]

With Brenner, a total turnabout was achieved: The distinguishing feature of the Jews was to be the loss of any shred of uniqueness. They would be merely different from others in the same way that other peoples differ from each other. Other Zionist thinkers followed suit. Micha Joseph Berdichevsky, author and journalist, called for a complete break with the past and wanted to give full precedence to Jews over Judaism. The choice was simple: To be the last Jews or the first Hebrews. In order to be the first Hebrews, the Jews were entitled to break the chains and shackles of an outdated Judaism.[8]

Jacob Klatzkin placed every emphasis on uninhibited nationalism:

In longing for our land, we do not desire to create there a base for the spiritual values of Judaism. To regain our land is for us an end in itself—the attaining of a free national life. The content of our life will be national when its forms become national. Indeed, let it not be said that the land is a precondition for a national life; living on the land is ipso facto the national life.[9]

Between these two extreme groups—retaining chosenness at all cost or denying it completely—moved the Zionist ideological pendulum in search of a balanced, middle road. In his speech opening the First Zionist Congress, Herzl declared that "Zionism means a return to Judaism even before the return to the land of the Jews." Such a declaration was required from a political point of view, if only to quell religious suspicions and to form a united framework in which all Zionists could find a place. But Herzl, like Nordau, Weizmann, and Jabotinsky, did not lend substance to such declarations. None of them indicated how the unique destiny would find expression in the state to come.

The answer was given in many ways. The great majority of Zionists wanted to preserve a certain Jewish quality which would define their future society. Two themes recur: the need for adherence to Jewish heritage, and the singularity of the future state as an exemplary model society. The link between these two themes is not clear. The view was utopian and almost always included a reference to the "vision of our prophets," side by side with lofty ideas of social justice. But the specific Jewish content was eroded by the weight of hyperbole. Lofty social ideas and Isaiah's prophecy of universal peace embellished Zionist speeches, but these could have served any highly motivated society.

In fact, what happened in Palestine was a constant process of political compromise which permitted the largely urban population to retain some Jewish customs and tradition. Naturally, they paid little attention to an issue as remote as the future state's position vis-à-vis the nations of the world. In Labor Zionism a different process took place. There, a conscious attempt was made to cast a new content into the old mold. The workers' parties adopted a credo which was not content with

Jewish sovereignty, with being a mere nation among nations, or even with an "exemplary society." Zionist socialism regarded itself as the legitimate heir of biblical ideas and prophetic visions. Israel would indeed become a "treasure nation"; but in a modern context, this meant the new workers' society embodying the highest goals of Zionist socialism.

It is beyond the scope of this book to examine the manifold factions and movements of socialist Zionism which left their indelible mark on the extraordinary and impressive history of the Labor movement. Suffice it say that Mapai, the dominant party, under the leadership of Ben Gurion, saw Jewish choseness as intertwined with the socialist message. The revolutionary fervor of the pioneers of the Second and Third Aliyot—founders of the Histadrut and Labor's economic and social infrastructure—was the Palestinian successor to Jewish revolutionary tendencies in Eastern Europe. Out of this combination of revolution and nationalism, Labor's new tree of life emerged. Within this labor environment, the international links and the posture toward the outside world acquired a special meaning: While political Zionism revolutionized Jewish existence by the adoption of prevailing notions of political self-determination, the Labor movement endeavored to translate the Jewish terms of uniqueness into a contemporary universal language.

Labor philosophy was not satisfied with mere liberation from past shackles and a break with the Jewish tradition which praises the Lord "who has not made us like the peoples of the earth"; it sought to go further and place the new Israel at the helm of international society, pointing the way to a new Jerusalem where equality and brotherhood prevail. The role of traditional scripture and prayer books was replaced by new writings which spoke with messianic passion about a new millennium: a classless society, the religion of work, the redemption of man, the communal settlement experience, the kibbutz and the moshav, the Histadrut as a workers' society. The pretense was immense: Israel, said labor ideologist Nachman Syrkin, "will redeem the world which crucified him; Israel will once again become the chosen of the peoples!"[10] This was a new prophetic statement transplanting the ancient spirit into a contemporary, secular and social context.

Ben Gurion—both as Yishuv leader and as Israel's first prime minister—gave this notion a popular expression. He insisted that the "Jewish nation is not a mere national and political entity but embodies a moral will and bears a historical vision since the moment it made its appearance on the stage of history." And he continued:

Not helpless longings for the tales of an imaginary past but a tense expectation of a perfect future and a vision of the universal rule of justice and peace is the historical philosophy which we inherited— and through us, the whole world inherited—from the prophets of Israel. This expectation, this belief in the future, stood us in our days of persecution and adversity, and it is this which brought us here, to the very beginning of our national redemption in which you will also find the first sparks of a universal human redemption.[11]

Socialist Zionism thus turned a full circle. The Jews who were pushed out of history—into a "historical corner," to use Ahad Ha'am's phrase—return to it as a latter-day guide to the perplexed. The message which the new Jews bore was a new kind of redemption—not divine grace but a social gospel; not a messiah to come but messianic action now. If political Zionism sought to return Israel as a normal nation to the international fold and thus establish equality on a national basis, Labor Zionism wanted to turn Israel into a moral leader. A social duty replaced religious devotion; a universal commitment replaced the old Covenant. Labor Zionism retained the tradition of messianic chosenness and indeed many refer to its teachings as "secular missianism."

Religious Zionism, a minority group within the Zionist movement and the Yishuv, certainly could not accept such substitutes to Mosaic law and traditional Jewish thought. Such substitutes—national as well as socialist—ignored the very foundations of Judaism and dismembered, in religious eyes, the one argument through which the Jews could claim Zion as theirs. Religious Zionism was ready to make a compromise with secular Zionists, to belong to their organizations and to coexist with them politically—much to the fury of the big, non-Zionist Orthodox camp. They were not ready to compromise their very credo. Nevertheless, there was no better proof of the intensity of the Zionist craving for normalization than the universalist attitude adopted by the leaders of religious Zionism.

Until the Six-Day War—that watershed event—Israel's status among the nations did not particularly trouble the leaders of Hamizrachi and Hapoel Hamizrachi, the religious and labor-religious Zionist movements. They accepted the political aims of secular Zionism, including the return to the family of nations within the framework of a secular nation state. Their interest lay inward, and their goals were defined within the Zionist movement and the Yishuv's political, social, and settlement problems. They acted for their own religious interests and way of life without posing a question mark on the striving for international equality. On the contrary, in the period preceding the 1967 war, the religious parties exercised a restraining and moderating influence on Israel's foreign and defense policy. And although Hamizrachi's vote in the 1903 Zionist Congress, which supported the Uganda plan—the "night shelter" intended to temporarily replace Zion—was not characteristic of their future policies, there were no signs in their policies and utterances of any isolationist chauvinism. When religious leaders and thinkers expressed themselves on Israel's external dimension—again, before that traumatic war—their words bore the message of humanism and universalism bequeathed by enlightened Zionism. This was also true for the religious precursors of Herzl's Zionism. Rabbi Zvi Hirsch Kalischer, who published his famous pamphlet, *Drishat Zion,* calling for the Return to Zion in 1862, saw in it the beginning of Redemption in the traditional sense but simultaneously imbued it with political and practical viability and drew inspiration from the na-

tional independence which the Bulgarians wrested from the
Ottoman Empire. Like political Zionists, Kalischer, too,
thought that the restoration of independence and the return to
agriculture would improve Israel's image among the Gentiles, a
sentiment to be reflected years later by Herzl's *Die Judenstaat*.

Rabbi Moshe A. Amiel, chief rabbi of Tel Aviv in Mandatory
Palestine and one of Hamizrachi's ideological leaders, explained religious Zionism in terms which seem incredible in
our days of Gush Emunim zealotry:

> Internationalism in Judaism is not only a conclusion but the very con-
> cept which gave birth to our ideology, our alpha and our omega. . . .
> There is no greater historical forgery than that which limits Judaism to
> vulgar and simplistic nationalism whose only foundation is nothing
> more than the urge to exist and the egotistical impulse which is part of
> every creature.[12]

And while the Nazis were trampling over Europe and murdering the Jews, he wrote:

> Judaism's outlook is pure, even extreme, internationalism. After all,
> our history begins not with the Patriarchs but with Adam. . . . Our
> Torah is not content with nationalism alone but has regard for the
> whole world and general humanity precedes our Patriarchs. . . . and
> our holidays, including the Sabbath, have not only a national char-
> acter but also a universal human nature and are founded not only on
> historical national events but also on the nature common to all
> dwellers of this earth.

Rabbi Amiel went on to blame secular Zionism for drawing its
"inspiration not from God's image in man but from the Gentiles' hatred of the Jews, while our religious ideology draws on
love—Israel's love of God and of every human being created in
His image."[13]

Another well-known rabbi, Yehuda Ashlag, wrote in 1940:
"The peace of the world precedes the Ingathering of the Exiles.
In other words, as long as self-love and egotism reign among
nations, the sons of Israel too will not be able to worship the

Almighty."[14] He explained that Israel was not able to inherit its ancestors' land without a universal observance of the rights of minorities and the liberties of the individual, a condition precedent for world peace.

A far cry from the rhetoric of the extremist religious groups which began to dominate the Israel scene after 1967! Yet these excerpts demonstrate how ready the religious-Zionist segment was to accept the general assumptions of Zionism and how removed it was from any trace of Jewish xenophobia and chauvinism.

The volte-face which took place within the religious camp after 1967 has no previous roots in the prestate period. Gush Emunim, and the philosophy which it represents, are all the creation of the post-independence period. Let us, therefore, examine now how the idea of normalization withstood the test of events which led the Yishuv toward the fulfilment of Herzl's dream. Our first examination leads us to the Zionist endeavor to establish a foothold in the Middle East.

4

EASTWARD TO ZION

INHERENT in the Zionist awakening, from its earliest days, was a certain duality. Zionism came into being in Europe and sought to return the Jews to the Middle East. "We are foreigners, outcast foundlings, unwanted guests in Europe," declared Lilienblum, one of the founders of the "Lovers of Zion" in Russia:

In the heyday of religion, we were strangers in Europe because of our faith, and now with the ascent of nationalism, we are strangers because of our race. Yes, we are Semites within Aryans, the sons of Shem within the sons of Japhet, a Palestinian tribe from Asia within the lands of Europe. . . . Yes, we are strangers and strangers we shall be forever.

And Lilienblum ended his exhortation by a call to go East, to the "unforgotten land of our ancestors."[1]

In the East stood the cradle of Jewish civilization. In the East, stood Jerusalem and the Wailing Wall; in every synagogue "East" is where the Ark and the Holy Scrolls of the Torah are—the side pointing toward Zion, symbolizing an age-old craving. The Jews in their western Diaspora could never, despite their long ancestry in Europe, forget their eastern origin. When they wanted to forget this, there were enough anti-Semites around to remind them of their Semitic, foreign origin. Moreover, Zionism drew inspiration, at least partially, from other national liberation movements which emphasized the return to authentic, historical roots. For the Jews such a direction meant a return to that eastern civilization which molded their nation and to the country from which they were exiled.

In Eastern Europe especially, where to Jews Europe meant oppression and abject poverty, Zionism's awakening was tinged by a nostalgia for the East. In one of his early poems, Chaim Nachman Bialik, Zionism's poet laureate, greeted a migrant bird returning from the East with all the pangs of longing for the "warm lands" of the Bible. In his short novel *Whither?* the Hebrew writer, M. Z. Feierberg, describes the torment of a young Russian Jew, who has forsaken the old ways without finding alternative solace. The book ends with this man delivering a sermon to a Zionist meeting in his township. Stunning in its verbal power, this sermon links the Return to Zion to momentous global events and to the ongoing conflict between East and West. The Second Temple and the bondage to the Romans is interconnected with a global change in which the East lost out to the new western power. With the fall of the East, the people of Israel fell. Now the tables were turned:

Europe is sick; everybody senses that its foundations are rotten and its society crumbling. Our destiny lies in the East. I do know that a day shall come when the hundreds of millions of people who live in the East, these dry bones, will come to life, will rise to their feet, a mighty host; then the East will reawake and will rule the world, replacing western hegemony.... Then new vigorous peoples will emerge and will establish the new society ... and you, my brethren, when you go now eastward, you must always remember that you are Oriental by birth ... that the worst enemy of the Jews is the West and that, therefore, it is unnatural that we, the Hebrew, Oriental people should put our lot with the nations of the West.... If it is true that the people of Israel have a mission, let them bear it and carry it to the Orient, not merely to Eretz Israel but the whole Orient.... My brethren, inscribe on your flag: Eastward! Eastward![2]

The hymn of the religious Zionist Hamizrachi movement ended with the same exhortation to go East. For many East European Jews, turning their back on Russia and Europe was accompanied by an idealization of the Orient. The age-long yearning for Zion, its sunny landscapes, deserts and orchards, was part of this vision which regarded the Jew as a captive of a hostile environment returning to his natural soil. The theme recurs in Zionist literature and as late as 1935, after a series of bloody conflicts between Jews and Arabs, Itamar Ben-Avi, a famous Hebrew journalist—the first Hebrew-speaking Sabra son to Eliezer Ben Yehuda, reviver of Hebrew—wrote:

We are Asians, because our land has always been an integral part of the greatest continent on this planet. . . . We are Asians because we have not come to a vacant land but to a populated region, part of whose inhabitants are doubtless remnants of the old Hebrews who converted to Islam and Christianity after the destruction of the temple.[3]

Israel Belkind, a First Aliyah early settler, clung to a similar view:

It is certain that among the Palestinian Arabs, we meet a great number of our own people who had been severed from us for the last fifteen hundred years. . . . Based upon these facts, we shall determine our attitude to them, and it is clear that our relationship can be only that of brothers. Not only brothers in the political sense—since history decrees that we share the same state together—but also brothers to the same race, the sons of the same nation.[4]

And in 1914, Nahum Sokolov, president of the Zionist organization, in an interview with the Egyptian journal *El Muq'atem* expressed his view in favor of a joint Arab-Jewish effort to build "a great Palestinian civilization which will replace the civilization of the earlier era."

In those same years, Yitzchak Ben Zvi, who would become president of Israel, was busy searching for traces of the ancient Hebrews among the Bedouins, and he found evidence of Jewish tribes who assimilated into the local Moslem inhabitants of Kurdistan and Afghanistan.

All these were expressions of one extreme view. However, there has always been in Zionism an opposite view which regarded Zionism as bringing western enlightenment to an underdeveloped region. Herzl's *Altneuland* is wholly European. And Nordau, in response to the Orientalist outlook, claimed that Zionist realpolitik dictates an alignment with Great Britain and the West and warned against a patronizing attitude toward the Arabs.

Jabotinsky, a totally committed westerner, recalled that the culture of the Yishuv was principally western and expressed his relief that "Ishmael is not our uncle."

Thus from the early days of Zionism, two differing conceptions can be discerned as to the cultural-political orientation of the state to come in Eretz Israel. When the pioneers of the early Aliyot began to settle the land, the Oriental inclination seemed in control.

Palestine was the Orient. Its sights and smells were not alien to the pioneers because the Bible is replete with them. When in 1912, the painter Reuven Rubin traveled as a young man of eighteen from Jaffa to Jerusalem, breathless excitement filled his heart: "It was truly wondrous in my eyes that everything seemed so familiar, as if I knew every rock, every tree, every desolate hillside. When the train arrived in Jerusalem, I felt that I was coming back home."[5] And he rushes to be photographed, as was the custom of many Zionist immigrants at that time, in Arab dress and headgear.

The new land was desolate and forsaken. Only small patches of greenery dotted its wide wastelands and a few villages pockmarked its marshlands. But in the fervent eyes of the pioneers, as well as in their literature, the country gloried in all its biblical beauty. The wishful heart took over from the objective eye. The first songs written in Palestine by the new pioneers adoringly depicted its Oriental visage: the "ululation of jackals at night"; the "shepherd's flute singing to descending herds of sheep"; the "flute's melancholy song like a breeze touching a blossoming orchard"; the "desert into which one is carried by slow pacing camels, on whose necks great bells will ring."

In Palestine the young European settlers met with Oriental

Jews, members of the Old Yishuv, and with newcomers from around the world who came to Eretz Israel upon hearing the call of Zionism. But it was the encounter with the local Arabs which was the most significant and which encouraged the Orientalist tradition among the new pioneers.

Isaac Epstein, a teacher, created a stir in 1907, when he published an article, "An Invisible Question," on the future relations between Jews and Arabs in Palestine.[6] Epstein charged that the Zionists were oblivious to the Arab question and were turning a blind eye to the existence of strong nationalistic feelings among the Arab inhabitants of Palestine. Since then, it has become customary to claim that Zionism, in its initial phases, was unaware of another people in the ancestral homeland. But this allegation was only partially true.

No one within the Zionist camp—or indeed outside it—perceived the force of the impending collision between the two national movements. Perhaps such blindness was Zionism's fortune, as an early realization of forthcoming events would have discouraged those who needed every iota of courage for routine existence. However, even before the Young Turks' revolution against Sultan Abdul Hamid in 1908—a date which usually marks the first signs of Arab nationalism—Zionist leaders addressed the Arab question in general and the attitude of Palestinian Arabs to Jewish immigrants in particular. The Zionist response was, to say the least, inadequate: It was naive in the sense that it did not estimate correctly the full measure of the Arab-Moslem violent rejection of any foreign presence on a piece of land which they regarded as wholly Arab.

Zionist leaders were thinking in Western European terms and emphasized the benefits to the Arabs from the Zionist enterprise. This attitude ran through the early phase of Zionist thinking, from the early founding days to the beginning of the British Mandate in Palestine. It retained its hold even in the face of growing Arab resistance. Thus, in Herzl's *Altneuland*, the Arab dignitary Rashid Bey praises the benign influence of the new society on all the inhabitants, Arab and Jew alike. In the same spirit, Herzl wrote to Yousuf Al'Khaldy: "The inhabitants ought to understand that they will gain excellent brothers and the Ottoman sultan will gain good and loyal citizens, who will turn the region into flourishing land."[7] In his memoirs Ben Gurion told that before World War I, he assumed the Arabs would receive the Zionist enterprise with open hands since it harbored prosperity for the country and all its dwellers.

So strong was this belief that it persisted—especially in the Labor movement—even in the face of continual Arab riots, and constant evidence of the Arabs' hatred of Zionism. In 1946, Mapam—the United Labor Party which was to the left of Ben Gurion's Mapai party—presented to the Anglo-American Inquiry Commission a memorandum advocating a binational state in Palestine. The proposal included the demand to open Transjordan to Jewish immigration and settlement:

We are convinced that when the Palestine problem is satisfactorily solved and when the Transjordanian Arabs are given a chance to see how their brethren across the river benefit from prosperity and progress, they shall willingly open the gates of Transjordan to Jewish settlement.[8]

Moreover, socialist Zionists had a "scientific" explanation for the frequent clashes with Palestinian Arabs and for their growing resistance to the Jewish presence. The conflict was merely another local product of a global "class struggle."

Ben Gurion's views were significant. Like many of his colleagues, and like the socialist ideologist Ber (Dov) Borochov, Ben Gurion believed that the local Arab fellahin were descended from the ancient Jews who in time of trouble and strife "preferred to deny their religion, rather than leave their homeland."[9] When these allegedly "Jewish" Arabs refused to make any compromises with the new Jews, Ben Gurion and his colleagues saw in this a typical "class struggle," in which the landed effendi class exploits the friction with the Jews in order to divert the attention of the masses from their real class interests.

On the other hand, a common interest—and a future common front—would unite Jewish and Arab workers. Eventually, class consciousness would prevail and only then would Arabs and Jews co-exist in their common land. Only later, after the bloody riots of 1929, in which whole families of Jews were slaughtered by Arab mobs, did Ben Gurion reluctantly change his mind. He began to fathom the depths of the Arab rejection and to relinquish orthodox Marxist explanations.

This sobering process would take place at a later stage. In the early period, before the true nature of Arab opposition to Zionism became sufficiently clear, the encounter with the Arabs of the land did not produce on the part of the Jews the type of conflict one would have expected. On the contrary, the Arab was the Semitic relative, a freshly rediscovered brother who has kept the family tradition and, in many respects, was regarded as a model for the new Jew.

The Yishuv's early literature is significant. It is devoid of any trace of hostility to, or suspicion of, the Arab; many authors filled their writings with empathy and admiration for the native-born, free-spirited, local Arabs. If the Jews sought a release from galut images and searched for their new, authentic identity, the distant relative rediscovered, the uninhibited Arab, was a figure worthy of emulation. This belief was shared by many early settlers and some went even further and advocated intermarriage with the Arabs as a means of a quick merger. Inevitably, the settlers encountered banditry and violence, but this did not diminish the image of the Arab fellah and Bedouin as an authentic resident of the land of the Bible, a successor to, and perhaps a descendant of, the biblical patriarchs.

Looking back, one is tempted to dismiss these expressions as the fancy of romantic orientalism, always a characteristic of newcomers to the Middle East. But the emotional intensity which attracted the young Jewish settlers to their future enemies cannot be overlooked. Moshe Smilansky, one of the first pioneer-authors wrote, under an Arab pen name—Hawaja

Mussa—a series of books depicting with love and adoration the life of the Palestinian Arabs. He was succeeded by a whole genre of similar literature. The Bedouins aroused a special interest. Their ways and customs, as nomadic shepherds, reminded the settlers of the biblical stories and lit up their eager imaginations. "Let us live like the Bedouins!" exclaimed Meir Wilkansky, one of the stalwarts of the Second Aliyah. He saw the nomads as guides to the right way of life upon the land. The Arabs appeared as noble, proud people whose ways should be adopted by the settlers. Thus, for instance, Joseph Luidor, Brenner's author-friend who was assassinated with him by Arabs in 1921, described a young Hebrew, a native of the new land: "He was more friendly with the Arab boys and spent more time with them than with the Hebrew boys because among the Arabs he found boys after his own heart. For his Hebrew friends and their ways he had nothing but scorn and contempt."[10]

In fact such stories are not unlike actual biographies. Moshe Dayan, born on the first kibbutz to Second Aliyah parents, spent many of his childhood days with Arab boys whose re-sourcefulness, wisdom, and friendship he came to admire. A Bedouin boy, two years his senior, became a constant friend. When he was ten years old, he published a short story in the school paper in which he described an adventurous journey across the desert he and his two Arab friends, Ali and Mousta-pha, shared: They were attacked and the young Moshe Dayan was saved by his Arab friends and—as he wrote—"with the help of Allah and his Prophet Muhammad."[11]

Pesach Bar Adon, who later became a famous archeologist, assumed in the early twenties the Arab name Azis Effendi and joined a Bedouin tribe in their long trek across Palestine and Transjordan. And when Hashomer, the first Jewish self-defense organization formed prior to World War I, wanted to introduce sheepherding into the new settlements, three of its members lived among the Bedouins, sharing their life, wearing Bedouin dress, learning their ways.

The image of the new Jew in the literature of the early set-

tlers acquires an Oriental-Arab aspect which stands out against
the traditional image of the old Jew. He masters riding his Arab
horse, wears Arab headgear, and is unafraid of the Arabs. He
fights them, when necessary, and, therefore, they respect him
and accept him as one of their own. The old Arab name for
Jews, "sons of death," is not applicable to the new manly Jew.
One of the first stories written in Hebrew in the new land set
the tone. In "New Year for the Trees," a short story written in
1892, Ze'ev Yavetz described a boy who came from galut to
Petach Tikvah when he was six years old and whose physical
prowess was contrasted—as expected—with his brethren
across the sea. The boy "learns from the Arabs to accustom his
body to heat and frost, to flood and drought." In Jabotinsky's
short story, "A Little Jew," he told how a native-born, Arab-
speaking young boy leads him to an Arab village and through
his astuteness wins the respect of the dignitaries of the village.
Asked about his education, the young boy says that in his
Russian village he heard from gentile children that the Jews are
not a nation. Why? Because they cannot curse in their own
language and they cannot fight back when attacked. These two
deficiencies were now set right.[12]

The Arab in these and similar stories was the anti-Jewish goy
whom the new Jew sought to resemble. The Arab represented a
twofold need: to be released from the grip of galut and to become a goy. An extreme manifestation of this tendency is
found in one of the earliest Hebrew plays written in Palestine.
The play *Allah Karim* (an Arabic title) was written by Levy-
Ariyeh Orloff-Arieli and was published in 1912 in *Hashilo'ah*,
the main Zionist organ in Russia. It depicts a group of young
pioneers from the Second Aliyah, who live, as was the custom
of those days, in a commune under the photographs of an un-
likely, but then common, pair—Herzl and Marx.

Naomi, the heroine, rebuffs the love of two members of the
commune, all of whom are depicted as soul-searching, helpless
creatures. She prefers Ali, an Arab boy vendor. When one of the
pioneers kills an Arab, Ali avenges his slain friend by killing the

pioneer. But even this deed does not change Naomi's love for Ali, and the play ends with an amazing, tempestuous monologue in which she renounces the commune: "My soul despises you, civilized worms! From the wild Arab I have learned something. He taught me the words 'Allah Karim.'. . . I have chosen the way of life and war! 'Allah Karim,' God is merciful!"[13] Such sentiments naturally expressed an extremist mentality, but they embodied an authentic nucleus. Israel returned to the Orient, and the Arab was the true son of the East, the authentic representative of healthy rootedness, the native-born who stood in total contrast to "civilized worms." Indeed, pro-Arab literature in Palestine reached such dimensions that *Hashilo'ah*, edited in Odessa by Ahad Ha'am, carried an article in 1907 by Dr. Joseph Klausner, who scolded the Palestinian writers "who portray all Jews in Palestine as Arab-speaking and Arab look-alikes."[14]

But in spite of these literary expressions, reality took its own independent course. Clashes with the Arab farmers and workers, whose livelihood was often endangered by the same pioneers who insisted on "Hebrew self-work," became more menacing. The Hebrew literature of the time contains many admonitions against any exploitation, any step which might adversely affect the local Arabs. In 1907 Rabbi Binyamin (the pen-name of Joshua Feldman-Reddler) published in a London-based Hebrew periodical edited by Brenner a sermon in biblical style addressed to the Jews of Palestine, which ended with an explicit commandment: "Thou shalt love the Arab dweller of the land for he is your brother, a flesh of your flesh and thou shalt not close your eyes to him."[15]

This book does not deal with the history of the Arab-Jewish conflict but only with the role played by the Arabs within Zionist consciousness and their impact on the new Jews' quest for a new "normalized" identity. From this point of view, this quest cannot be regarded as merely denoting a fashionable romanticism; it had acquired a new dimension: a true search for a substitute to the European-Jewish roots which, ostensibly at least, were cut by the revolutionary act of leaving Europe and creating a new Jew.

The First World War marked the beginning of the end of this hankering eastward. The Yishuv was divided between the pro-British Nili underground and those who, like Ben Gurion and future President Ben Zvi, had cast their lot with the Ottoman Empire. But with the British conquest of Palestine during World War I a new era began. The post-war Aliyot brought not only pioneer settlers but thousands of Jews who preferred urban life. The Balfour Declaration and the terms of the British Mandate, commanding Britain to allow free immigration of Jews to their destined National Home, accelerated and exacerbated Arab resistance to the growing Jewish presence. Pro-Arab ideology was gradually eroded by the harsh facts of strife. To the Arabs, the Mandate policy was a perennial object of opposition. Consequently, the Jews had to be ever alert to prevent Britain's betrayal, and the Arab began to lose his heroic-biblical aura. He became a hostile and unrepentant enemy, whose leaders attacked Zionism in vitriolic language and pressured Britain to revoke its policy toward the Jewish settlement of Palestine.

And yet, notwithstanding these harsh facts, the former mood managed to survive—especially within Labor Zionism. When the Histadrut—that unique combination of trade unions, worker-owned enterprises, and a social-educational network—was established in 1921, one of its first decisions was to establish an Arab Workers Union and to cooperate with Arab working classes. Thus class interests would cut across national barriers put up by the scheming effendis. The workers' cooperation would build bridges linking the two Semitic relatives. In 1927, the Histadrut decided upon a "joint organization" in which Arab workers were to participate with Hebrew workers. All these efforts bore meager fruit, but at one point the Histadrut managed to crown its endeavors with a strike of both Arab and Jewish railway employees.

The literature of the period between the two World Wars

lacks the Oriental enthusiasm of Ottoman days but occasionally retains its strong East-Arab orientation and, despite the
growing bloodshed, never includes a word of hate or animosity
toward the Arab. Thus, in a story by Yacov Rabinovitch, a
Hebrew *shomer*, a guard defending a settlement against Arab
marauders, thinks aloud about his wish to live like a Bedouin.
Intertwined with this wish is the question: "Have we come
here to create a life of our own spirit or to return to Ishmael and
Lot?"[16]

The yearning toward the Arab, Oriental, and Mediterranean
ambience expressed itself also in the art and music of the
Yishuv. The painter Abel Pan (né Fefferman), who came to the
Bezalel Academy of Jerusalem a short time after World War I, is
representative of the school which sought to create an indigenous art form, unlinked to western fashions. His paintings,
depicting biblical figures in the guise of local Arabs, embody
this tendency as do the early paintings of other artists—Nahum Gutman, Moshe Kastel, and Reuven Rubin.

Among the composers, who arrived in Palestine laden with a
European musical education, a conscious effort was made to
listen and give voice to the sounds of new Oriental reality and
to its singular melodies and tempos. Thus, Paul Ben Haim
arrived in Palestine in the thirties, having established a reputation in his native Germany. But the new land left its mark
upon his Palestinian works in their Oriental melodies and or-
chestration. In the works of Uriah Alexander Boskovitch, the
Oriental influence reaches new heights in such works as the
concerto for violin, which includes an original theme based on
a Bedouin melody and the "Semitic Suite," the very name of
which attests to its musical connotations. This is also true of
other works, such as Menachem Avidom's "Mediterranean Sym-
phony" and Abel Ehrlich's "Bashrav," which ignored western
tonality and was entirely written in Oriental-Arab scale.

But gradually reality manifested itself. The Yishuv's leaders
began to comprehend the depth of the Arabs' incorrigible resistance to Jewish attempts to control any part of Palestine. Re-

luctantly, and much to its chagrin, the Hebrew Yishuv began to recognize the rising tide of Arab nationalism and its uncompromising determination to see the whole of Palestine as part of an Arab-Moslem domain. Beyond the Zionists' own internal disputes on the Arab issue loomed a wall of unmitigated rejection in which the Jews were looking vainly for a crack. Even the most moderate elements in the Yishuv, such as Judah Magnes's Brit Shalom movement for Arab-Jewish understanding, which was ready to relinquish Jewish sovereignty, could not reach an understanding with the Arabs. Thus, a local Palestinian Arab leader responded to the advances of one of Brit Shalom's spokesmen:

I shall tell you quite frankly that I would rather deal with somebody like Jabotinsky than with you. I know that Jabotinsky is our unremitted enemy and that we have to fight him, while you seem to be our friend. But truly I do not discern a difference between your goal and that of Jabotinsky. You also stick to the Balfour Declaration, to the National Home, to unlimited immigration, to Jewish purchase of Arab land—everything which for me is an issue of life and death.[17]

Similarly, one of the leaders of the Arab Istiqlal (independence) party wrote in response to Dr. Magnes's proposals which renounced the idea of a Jewish state and sought to establish a limited autonomy for the Jewish community in Palestine:

In your opinions and proposals I can see nothing but a blatant provocation against the Arabs, who will allow nobody to share with them their natural rights . . . as to the Jews, they have no rights whatsoever except spiritual memories replete with catastrophes and woeful tales. . . . It is, therefore, impossible to have a meeting between the leaders of the two peoples—the Arab and the Jewish.[18]

All attempts at cooperation or cultural dialogue were swept aside by such Arab moods. The efforts of the Histadrut to have a binational workers cooperative crashed against the wall of Arab rejection. Within Labor there were a few holdouts: In 1931 Chaim Arlozoroff, head of the Jewish Agency political department—whose murder a few years later would ignite a near civil war between left and right within the Yishuv—still declared that coexistence and true self-interest would bring about a cooperation between Arab and Jewish workers. He still believed that Arab leaders would see the light and appreciate the benefits accruing to them from cooperation with the Yishuv. After the outbreak of the Arab riots in 1936, even such pious hopes disappeared in the gunfire and smoke.

Worse still was the fate of the Jews' attempt to return to their eastern origins, to establish a bridge with Oriental tradition, and to merge their culture with that of their Semitic cousins. The Arabs never accepted this idea of Orientalism. When the Second Aliyah settlers arrived, the Arabs nicknamed them "Muscob" (Muscovites), as a label defining their inferior strangeness. In the beginning of the British occupation, the Arabs often alleged that the Jews were German spies only to change to a persistent charge that the Zionists were communist agents and Bolshevik spies.

In 1937, Jamal Husseini, secretary of the Higher Arab Committee, appearing before the British Royal Commission on Palestine, described the Palestinian Jews as foreign agents who carried with them into the Moslem Middle East the dangerous virus of communism:

As to the communistic principles and ideas of Jewish immigrants, most repugnant to the religion, customs, and ethical principles of this country, which are imported and disseminated, I need not dwell upon them as these ideas are well known to have been imported by the Jewish community.[19]

Ironically, at that time the Yishuv was virtually ostracizing the small communist party, which was in sympathy with the Arab cause!

In the eyes of the Palestinian Arab leaders the Jews were not merely strangers. From the beginning of the British Mandate they invoked the language of Christian anti-Semitism as a

weapon against the Yishuv. To the traditional anti-Jewish elements in the Qur'an and Islamic tradition, they now added a
modern ingredient borrowed from Europe: The Jews were the
microbes of death and doom and carried with them the destruction of their host states. In his testimony before the British Royal Commission on Palestine in 1936, Ouni Abdul Hadi,
leader of the Istiqlal party, charged that the Jews were a nation
of usurers and added that if sixty million Germans could not
bear the presence of six hundred thousand German Jews, how
could the Palestinian Arabs be expected to accept the presence
of four hundred thousand Jews in a much smaller country. To
the Jews of the Yishuv, such expressions, deriving their inspiration from Nazi Germany, bore the only-too-familiar seeds
of an ancient hatred which they never dreamed would take
root in the new soil.

In vain did the Zionists try to prove to the Arabs that they
were not dealing with the old Jews but with the new Hebrews
who saw in the Arabs long-separated members of the same
family. At first, the Arab leaders were still trying, for tactical
purposes, to draw a distinction between western foreign Jews
and their "own" Oriental Jews with whom, so the legend goes,
they lived in peace and harmony. But soon even that claim was
dropped and it remains as a relic in the Palestine Liberation
Organization's notorious covenant which allows the Jews who
resided in Palestine before 1917 to remain behind, and all the
other Jews to be expelled from Arab Palestine. In their verbal
and actual war against the Yishuv and the state, the Arabs no
longer made any distinction between Oriental and Western
Jews.

In the history of the Yishuv, at least since the Balfour Declaration, a total Arab rejection drenched all Zionist hopes of
turning eastward. The very idea of a Jewish presence in Palestine, any Jewish presence, was now an anathema which could
not even be contemplated. Single episodes, such as the short-
lived Weizmann-Feisal accord and Ben Gurion's futile dialogues with Palestinian Arab leaders, lost their significance in

the face of this rejection. In 1938, when His Majesty's Government covened the St. James Conference on Palestine as a prelude to its capitulation to Arab demands, the lines were clearly drawn. The Arab delegation, which included the representative of Arab states, refused to sit at the same table, even at the opening ceremony, with the Jewish delegation which was comprised of delegates from the Yishuv and from the Diaspora.

When Israel gained its national independence after a bitter war, the most brutal of all paradoxes took place. The newly created Israel absorbed hundreds of thousands of Jewish refugees from Arab-Muslim countries. Its demographic nature altered radically, and it became more Mediterranean, more Oriental than ever before. It was then that the Arabs, with the aid of their newly acquired power and wealth, unleashed a propaganda war of unprecedented magnitude against Israel in which the Jewish state was presented as the paradigm of white, European presence in the Middle East. The Arab anti-Semitic diatribe acquired a new Nazi-inspired ferocity. The notorious *Protocols of the Elders of Zion*, the czarist police's forged document, has been used throughout the Arab states against the descendants of those very Jews at whom it was originally aimed. A full circle was completed.

Zionism, which began with an attempt to redeem the Jews from Gentile-Christian hatred, crashed into the same reaction from the Arab-Moslem world. At the root of these two rejections lay two different reasons, but the similarity was too striking for Jews—both old and new—to disregard. The analogy between the two rejections was obvious. Zionism, like Jewish emancipation and assimilation in nineteenth-century Europe, wanted to retain only part of the Jewish tradition and was ready to discard that part which expressed Jewish exclusiveness and separated Judaism from the surrounding world. The assimilationists sought to achieve this on an individual level, the Zionists on a national level. In both cases, the attempt failed. The world they wanted to enter—Christian Europe and

Arab Middle East—was not ready to accept them as equal partners, either individually or as a nation-state. In both cases, the rejection was tainted by bigotry and racist prejudice. In both cases, the Jews tried to extend a friendly hand and were ready to make far-reaching compromises in order to achieve integration. In both cases there was no response. The enlightened assimilationists were ready to relinquish any facet of national allegiance, to renounce the Jewish "tribal" existence, to introduce extensive reforms into their religion to gain entrance to the civilized salons of Europe. Secular Zionism was ready to give up the traditional messianic element in Judaism, to exchange the traditional blessing "thou hast chosen us from the nations of the earth" with "to be a goy like all the goyim" to gain acceptance to the Middle East. But the concessions served no purpose: Jewish identification was forced upon Zionism, just as it was forced a hundred years before upon Jews seeking emancipation.

On examination this analogy is found wanting and flawed in many respects. Yet the Arab rejection of Israel—of any Jewish state—was bound to have a traumatic effect on Israel's national psyche. The two rejections could not be seen in isolation, and the tendency grew to regard them both as part of some invisible scheme which frustrated any attempt by Jews to shake off their singular fate.

The words of Israeli author and journalist Aharon Megged are illuminating in this respect. In his essay, "Bitter Thoughts," Megged somberly reflected on the failure of the Israeli attempt to win the hearts of the Arabs and on the obtuseness of the Arab mind toward the feelings and views of its Jewish adversary. Megged, who is labor-oriented and dovish in his thinking and express an empathy with the Arab, drew a comparison between the failure of German-Jewish assimilation and Israel's failure to win Arab acceptance. He quoted Professor Gershom Scholem, who described the one-way dialogue between German and Jew in the heyday of German Enlightenment:

The Jews' pleas and begging met with no response. When the Germans finally saw fit to hold some kind of dialogue, in a humanitarian spirit, it was based on the premise, explicit or implicit, of Jewish self-abnegation, of the advanced atomization of the Jews as a society in the process of disintegration.

With whom, then, did the Jews converse in this dialogue? They spoke to themselves. Many acted as if the echo of their own plea would suddenly become the voice of other people, so intensely desirous of hearing it were they. When they thought they were talking to the Germans, they were only talking to themselves.[20]

Megged compares this doomed attempt with Jewish-Arab experience:

How depressing it is to consider that exactly the same, almost word for word, could be said of the so-called dialogue we have been holding with the Arabs for the past sixty to seventy years. We kowtow with all the might of our sense of honor, and lack thereof, out of the hope that the echo of our cry will suddenly become the voice of someone else; and when we believe we are talking to the Arabs, we are only talking to ourselves . . . that is indeed a pathetic sight. It arouses sadness and compassion in equal measure, both in its German-Jewish revelation and in its Arab-Jewish context.[21]

What began as a march eastward, away from Jewish predicament, ended in the recesses of Jewish psyche as a new awareness of Jewish helplessness in the face of an imposed isolation. The dreams of integration into an Arab Middle East lay in ruins. In 1922, in the paper of the Legion of Work—a commune whose members shared the meager income from their hard manual work—there was a vision of the future Ein Harod, the kibbutz which was then being built in the valley of Jezreel. The article described the kibbutz in a hundred years, and the author dwelt on its prosperity and cultural achievements, as well as the "houses built in Oriental style." In the center of the kibbutz stands the sculptured monument: "Two men, a Jewish worker and an Arab worker, sit on a stone, holding a flag bearing the inscription 'Equality, Fraternity, Liberty.' "[22] Today, in Ein Harod stands Sturman House commemorating three generations of sons who fell in the country's war with the Arabs.

5

THE HOLOCAUST AND THE
STRUGGLE FOR ISRAEL'S
INDEPENDENCE

THE increasing friction with the Arab world in the late 1930s did not seem to the leadership of the Yishuv and the Zionist movement to endanger the Zionist concept of a two-fold Jewish return—to their land and to the world. Even when Britain betrayed the Mandate and the Balfour Declaration and in Europe the Nazi Beast was marching towards Auschwitz, the Zionist credo remained unshaken. In those days of torment—of impotent debates at the Evian Conference on Jewish refugees—when the world was closing its gates to Jewish refugees of Nazi terror, as if they were the carriers of some dangerous plague, Zionists remained constant in their devotion to Herzlian thought. There was anger. Clenched fists were waved at perfidious Albion, but there was no attempt to re-examine Zionism's basic assumptions.

The exacerbating conflict with the Arabs had put an end to the yearning eastward, but Zionist leaders still thought that the conflict could be localized and limited. In this context, Britain's betrayal was seen as the unjust, cynical machinations of a government and its politicians. When Chaim Weizmann realized the magnitude of Britain's treason, he could not contain himself: At the Twentieth Zionist Congress in 1937, as the lights were going out in Europe, he could not continue his speech and, overcome with emotion, burst out crying publicly. But Weizmann, lifelong friend of Britain that he was, assured the congress that the English people, unlike their government, still supported the Zionist cause. The dissidents, headed by Jabotinsky, protested Weizmann's timid response and wanted a total evacuation of European Jews, but they too sought Zionist integration into the world community and proposed that the future Jewish state become a dominion in the British Commonwealth.

In retrospect, one wonders at the absence of any signs of despair. Zionism's basic assumption—that it miraculously would put an end to anti-Semitism—was totally destroyed by the Nazis; its hope of saving the Jews before the imminent catastrophe was frustrated by a combination of evil and indifference. After years of Zionist activity and after the establishment of a truly model society, hatred of Jews reached unimaginable heights and the plight of Jews fell to an even more unimaginable nadir.

What must be understood, however, is that the full horror of the Nazi nightmare was not, and could not have been, realized at the time. The Zionists were preoccupied with political work: how to save the menaced Jews; how to fight Britain's policy and, at the same time, participate in her war effort; how to survive. Moreover, in her capitulation to Arab demands, Britain resorted to realpolitik—the need to placate the Moslem world on the eve of a world war. The Zionist movement refuted these arguments but refused to see in this betrayal a deeper significance.

Indeed, during the time when Europe's Jewry was being systematically slaughtered, Zionist ideology of normalization remained unchanged. The news from Europe caused heartbreak, fury, and a renewed attempt to open Palestine's doors to those who sought escape. Toward the end of 1942 when news from Europe about the mass murders reached Palestine, a delegation of Polish Jews turned, panic-stricken, to Yitzchak Greenbaum, the head of the Yishuv's Salvation Committee. They wanted desperately to draw attention to the danger of extermination and tried to make Greenbaum swear to act so that there "will not be one moment of peace and quiet until the slaughter is stopped and the remnants saved." Greenbaum's reaction was so stunning as to be unbelievable:

I told them: No, I shall not swear to it! The fate of the Jews in Europe may be the main issue but it is not the only issue which troubles us. And once again I spoke to them about our need to extract ourselves from the position of extraordinary people and be a nation like all other nations. Two thousand years of galut were enough. Let us be equal members in this world.[1]

These words are not really indicative of Zionist ideology. A normal nation and an "equal member in this world" would certainly not react—toward the other nations, toward its own people—in the way Greenbaum reacted. The normal and instinctive behavior would have been to give total precedence and attention to saving helpless Jews from the Nazi slaughter. But this irrelevant reaction by a dedicated and devoted Zionist demonstrates how deeply rooted was the Zionist concept of normalization: it remained unmoved, in its grotesque version, even in the face of the Holocaust.

By the end of the war, when the full horror became known, Zionist leaders doubled their efforts to open the closed gates of Palestine and save those who had escaped extermination. The heroic days of Exodus and illegal immigration, the anti-British underground and the political action, which finally culminated in the United Nations partition plan. But even then, instinctive pre-Holocaust reactions survived and asserted their irrelevancies. The old Jews, the galut Jews, so ran the insane legend, went like sheep to the slaughterhouse. They did not behave as the new Hebrews would have behaved—by fighting back, resisting the Nazis and saving their Jewish honor. The Yishuv's instinctive reaction to the Holocaust was to emphasize the few desperate Jewish uprisings against the Nazis. Not everybody betrayed the gospel. The partisans, the fighters of the Warsaw Ghetto, the Jewish resistance, saved the Jews from total humiliation. Hence, the day of remembrance to the six million dead is named Day of Holocaust and Heroism, and the monuments and museums put special emphasis on the courage of the Jewish resistance. How the helpless, unarmed Jews could have resisted remains unexplained. Why it was dishonorable to die in Auschwitz, without fighting back, is not elucidated. The old Zionist credo denouncing the galut passivity was instinctively applied to a situation which lies beyond human experience, to which there is no moral guide and in which standard criteria of honor are not applicable.

With their arrival in Palestine the first refugees to filter through Britain's infamous armada often encountered an oddly anachronistic reaction. When Ruzhka Korczak, one of the legendary figures of the Warsaw Ghetto revolt, told the Histadrut council, in her native Yiddish tongue, about the horrors of her experiences, Ben Gurion said that they were shocked and moved by the tale of woes, "although it was told in a foreign and jarring language."[2] The suggestion that Ruzhka Korczak be sent to America to alert public opinion to the plight of the Jewish refugees in Europe was rejected because she had not had enough of an Yishuv experience for such a mission. When the first films of Nazi atrocities were shown to a private group, and a stunned silence descended on the audience, Ben Gurion, mustering every iota of strength, broke the silence by telling about similar tragedies—of Armenians, of Russians, of gypsies. The Jews are not alone, he said; man's inhumanity to man has had other victims, too.

But these awkward manifestations of an ill-applied concept did not alter the one crucial lesson: Zionist insistence that the Jews are safe only in their own land, had received a most wrenching testimony. Although no Zionist could have foreseen the full scale of the horror, their urgent insistence on a home and shelter for a menaced people was prophetic. After the Holocaust, the long dispute between Zionists and non-Zionists disappeared. Zionism became the leader of all Jews. The formerly powerful Jewish anti-Zionists groups vanished, and the few relics, such as the American Council for Judaism, shriveled into insignificance. The substitutes to political Zionism—Ahad Ha'am's idea of a spiritual center, Magnes's concept of a binational state, anything short of full sovereignty—were rejected and disappeared into the limbo of vaguely remembered history.

On the other hand, the Holocaust raised some doubts around primary Zionist premises. After Auschwitz, it was impossible to deal with the specter of anti-Semitism according to the concepts laid down by Herzl in nineteenth-century Vienna. There was to be no more understanding of, or neutrality to, anti-Jewish bigotry. There was no more place for blaming the sufferings on the galut Jews; no more escaping from Jewish history into the cozy shell of normalization at all costs. The spoiled Hebrew son, the Sabra, would have to grapple with the reality of the Holocaust and with the meaning of Jewish history. The lessons of the world's indifference to Jewish suffering and its refusal to save their lives from the German genocidal machine could not be disregarded and had to be explained. Some re-examination of the old truisms had to be undertaken.

That re-examination did not occur overnight. The impact was not immediate but slow and cumulative. Many years passed before the Sabra's attitude toward the galut Jew changed from total negation to compassionate understanding. The attitude toward the outside world was not immediately affected by the new information about the West's deafening silence in an hour of great need.

In 1948 the State of Israel was born, clinging to the original Zionist vision. Independence was granted according to international law and with the assistance of the great majority of nations, including the big superpowers—all in accordance with Herzl's foresight. The drafters of Israel's Declaration of Independence in 1948 saw Israel in the image of the early Zionist congresses: a secular state based on Jewish national history; a model society embracing equality regardless of religion or race; a people inspired by the prophets' vision of justice to all; a dutiful member in the family of nations.

David Ben Gurion led the state in accordance with this political gospel: Unbearably hard indeed is the lot of the Jews, but the State of Israel will bring remedy to a two-thousand-year-old malady. Jewish national revival will put an end to the perverted relations between Jews and Gentiles. The Jewish people are indeed different in their history and culture, but their fate will be that of a normal nation. The roots of the Jewish malaise lie in their dispersion among other nations, but the Ingathering of the Exiles will cure this malaise. The Nazis devoured other people too. Israel must make up not only with the world but, first and foremost, with Germany itself. All that is not enough. Israel itself, in its social order and spiritual content, must become "a light unto the nations." The Jews in their land will again be a "treasure nation" in the secular sense of the world.

Israel's dawn was characterized by a unique situation—military weakness and strong international support (later to reverse completely). The new Jewish state acquired international fame and drew general admiration. And indeed, in many respects, its achievements were truly unparalleled. With this in mind, Ben Gurion outlined the philosophy underlying his policy:

In defining a new road toward a world of liberty, freedom, peace, justice and equality, there is no monopoly to big powers. . . . Small states can nowadays guide humanity in scientific, social, and spiritual progress. . . . With the establishment of our state we have become more than ever citizens of the world. Our national independence has placed our world citizenship on a solid base. Not because of unrootedness do we espouse these issues of humanity and are aware of its needs and problems but because we are equal partners in these needs and problems.[3]

And the first foreign minister, Moshe Sharett, lay down the rule governing the young state's orientation:

We have not come into our home from the four corners of the world in order to isolate ourselves and to be alone within it or in order to cut or weaken our links with other nations and with the great world of culture and progress. We do not see ourselves as merely another state in the Middle East. . . . If we have acquired during our sojourns and

dispersion a world vision and perspective, we do not intend to give
them up now.... This world perspective, regarding things through a
global vision, is not only our heritage from the days of sojourns and
dispersion. We believe it is from earlier times than that, because in
this vision will be found the quintessence of our ancient tradition,
before the sojourns and dispersion, which always emphasized the universal in our spiritual world and all which is supranational in our road
to morality and progress.[4]

These shades of *Altneuland* indicate clearly that in the first
years of independence there was no soul-searching re-examination of traditional Herzlian concepts. Current political need
and the effort to bring in and absorb hundreds of thousands of
people from East and West exhausted both physical and intellectual resources. Moreover, a world shocked by what the Nazis had perpetrated lent Israel unprecedented support and assistance. Both the Soviet Union and the United States supported
the fledgling state. Nazism was seen as a passing dark cloud of
crazed inhumanity. Even in those early years, there was talk
about cooperation with Adenauer's Germany. So all-encompassing was the basic idea of Zionism, so total was the desire
to have a normal state, that it refused to be veered from its
steady course even by Apocalypse.

Many years passed before Israeli writers and politicians would
speak about the need to revise this Zionist theory. Eliezer Liv-
neh wrote twenty years after independence that in a post-Holocaust world there was no return to Herzlian Zionism:

As of now, the attitude of the Jewish people to the outside world (and
perhaps also to itself) will not be as of yore. Zionist thinking before
1939–45 and Zionist thinking after that, are not one and the same
thing.... Is the civilized humanity which was seen by Moses Hess,
[Leo] Pinsker, Ahad Ha'am and Herzl the same humanity which was
seen by our generation? And can our self-understanding and the understanding of the tension between us and the Gentiles remain without change? Indeed, we may endanger our survival if we shall act
according to criteria and practical conclusions drawn in a former era,
before the monstrous light of the gas chambers went up.[5]

These words were written after the Six-Day War, that historical turning point in Israel's mood, and not in the period following the Holocaust and the War of Independence. In those years, Israel established strong links with the European Right, and her emissaries were treated with respect and admiration by circles not noted for their philo-Semitism. Those were the heydays of "Israeli first, Jewish later," of the Sabra cult, of the Canaanite movement. In those days, Israel established links with most countries and her very name was synonymous with Democracy, Liberty, Socialism. Over a million refugees found shelter and home in their new country.

For Zionism it was a singular moment. Herzl's dream had become a reality.

6

THE SIX-DAY WAR: AN IDEOLOGICAL WATERSHED

THE ideological and practical ramifications of the Six-Day War were so all-encompassing in Israeli thinking and politics that there is justification for regarding it as a turning point in Zionist and Israeli history.

To understand the nature of this turnabout a reconstruction of its background is necessary. The June war was preceded by a period of national anxiety, such as Israel had not known since the days of the War of Independence. The Arab forces seemed, on the eve of the war, to menace the very existence of the state and the lives of its inhabitants. Moreover, this threat descended upon Israel unexpectedly, after years of believing that the status quo with the Arabs would be longlasting. This anxiety was compounded by the shock at the impotent apathy on the part of the international community in the face of Nasser's aggression. Within hours, international guarantees of Israeli free navigation sank into the waters of the blocked Tiran Straits and the United Nations observers' force vanished into thin Sinai air. Anxious Israelis followed with a mixture of contempt and fury the Security Council's perfidy and its cynical refusal to say one word which could be interpreted as a condemnation of the Arabs' blatant and openly declared attempt to strangle Israel.

Abba Eban described the sensations of Israelis on those fateful days: "As we looked around us we saw the world divided between those who were seeking our destruction and those who would do nothing to prevent it."[1]

Remembering the days in which Europe's Jews encountered a similarly divided world, Israelis would not soon forget those days of clenching fists and pounding hearts.

As a result of the war the land which until then lay beyond the impenetrable armistice line was reunited with Israel: Old Jerusalem, the Jewish Quarter lying in ruins, the Wailing Wall, Rachel's Tomb, Samaria and Judea—the sites and places whose very names evoked biblical connotations and past memories. The press reported that when the paratroopers reached the Wailing Wall, they—the symbol of Sabra toughness—wept on the ancient stones, the relic of past Jewish greatness and the destination of age-old longings.

In the religious sector, this encounter with holy places gave the war a new messianic meaning. Within a short time, a strong movement seeking to settle Judea and Samaria began to take root inside the religious camp, thus signaling a radical change in the traditionally moderate National Religious Party. The June war, by bringing Israel in touch with these cradles of Judaism, was for many religious Israelis the commencement of a new era. Religious thinkers and rabbis did not hesitate to see in Israel's victory a divine miracle. A profusion of religious writings argued the case for regarding the crushing of Israel's enemy, the liberation of the Wailing Wall, and Temple Mount as God's hand in action.

To the nonreligious sector, too, these were great days. Anxiety gave way to exhilaration, peril to euphoria. The siege was lifted and beyond the barbed wire lay the enchanted lands to which no Israeli could be indifferent. Within Israel the war unleashed a national debate as to the aims and goals of Zionism and its relationship with Judaism. A new sense of history began to permeate the public debate and the words "Jewish fate" became almost ubiquitous. The need to go back to the original Jewish sources, to return to the roots, was constantly heard. The Sabra paratroopers' weeping at the Wailing Wall—true or alleged, nobody knew—became an enduring legend.

To Meir Roston, Professor at Bar Ilan University, these tears

proved that "after generations of intellectual rational education, after years of consistent secularism, Israeli youth seeks
faith and the soul of its culture. The intellect becomes banal—
the spiritual link renews its attraction."[2] Since the war, a new
movement of repentants, or born again Jews, became widely
publicized and the mass media celebrated the conversion to
Orthodox religious life of famous Israelis—ex-kibbutzniks, air
force pilots, and show business people. The transmutation of
pop stars from hashish and sex to yeshiva and synagogue became a regular feature of the popular press. This movement
included many authentic and moving stories of men and
women who found peace of mind and a true vocation by turning to religion; often they were presented as indicative of a new
repentant mood which had allegedly descended on secular Israelis and of their wish to return to the religious sources of
Judaism. But the war had not brought about a renaissance of
religious observance. For a fleeting moment, the emotion-
laden encounter with the biblical cradles of Jewish civilization
was clothed with religious sentiments. But aside from the natural reaction of any Jew coming face to face with the relics of
the Jerusalem built by King David and King Solomon, the excitement subsided leaving behind it no substantial religious
residue.

On the contrary, the postwar period which, until the 1973
Yom Kippur War, was characterized by an economic boom and
a sharp rise in the standard of living marked a growing materialism and hedonistic permissiveness in Israeli society. It was
this new public mood and not a religious awakening that
marked the true change in Israel.

The stunning victory, sharp and quick as a surgeon's scalpel,
which came in the wake of menace and fear, created a mood of
exuberance. The adjective "invincible" was prefixed as a matter of routine to the name Israel. The country became, in the
eyes of its beholders, a mighty military power which the Arabs
could not conquer. "No one can budge us from staying forever
on the Suez," said General Ariel Sharon a short time before the

Yom Kippur War, "and our hold on the canal disintegrates Egypt from within."[3] And Yitzchak Rabin explained that the defense lines along the canal radically altered Israel's strategic posture, "because its military might will be sufficient to prevent the other side from undertaking any military initiative."[4] Military experts reinforced the view that the postwar status quo was preferable to all other alternatives and that no one could upset it. Five months before the outbreak of the Yom Kippur War, Yigael Yadin, ex-chief-of-staff, said: "I do not believe that in our generation there will be another war like those of 1948 and 1967. This is one of the successes of the Six Day War."[5]

These statements nourished a new mood of self-confidence. "The world," which betrayed Israel in its dark days, was not entitled to tell it what to do and how to behave. Self-reliance was Israel's only weapon.

The consequence of this new mood was a gradually growing friction with the outside world and with Western public opinion. Immediately after the war, Israel enjoyed wide international support which enabled her in September 1967 to repel an Arab-Soviet motion at the United Nations calling for a total Israeli withdrawal to the prewar lines. In November 1967 the Security Council accepted the famous Resolution 242, which many Israelis rightly regarded as an Israeli achievement and which Jerusalem endorsed. In Khartoum, the Arabs issued their three nos—no to peace, no to negotiations, no to recognition—vis-à-vis Israel; African nations, except for one, maintained their strong links with Israel. But with Israel consolidating control of the territories conquered in the war, with the proliferation of settlements there, and with increasing Arab economic strength, the conflict with her Western and Third World friends was constantly exacerbated. As the years passed, and within the country the ideas of "Greater Eretz Israel"—which contend that Judea, Samaria, and Gaza are part of Israel—acquired more political support, the Jewish state met harsher reactions from outside. The Security Council, never a friend, adopted an almost Pavlovian reaction to anything concerning Israel and habitually issued one-sided condemnations. Public criticism in the western press grew. Third World countries became restless. The politics of this new situation called for the same cool assessment which had guided Ben Gurion in the difficult fifties.

But in postwar Israel, just awakened from nightmarish fears into euphoric reality, the confrontation with the world heralded a new significance for Israel: it inherited the mantle of the rejected Jew, differing only in its ability to be defiant. This ideology started in hubris—Israel the invincible—and terminated in despair—Israel the pariah state. This overbearing attitude found expression in a popular song of the period which topped the hit parade at the time. Entitled "The Whole World Is Against Us," the song begins:

> The whole world is against us.
> This is an ancient tale
> Taught by our forefathers
> To sing and dance to.

Having thus established the link between the persecution of the Jews and Israel's isolation, the song goes on to establish the difference between the forefathers and the Sabra sons:

> If the whole world is against us,
> We don't give a damn.
> If the whole world is against us,
> Let the whole world go to hell.[6]

The same mood invaded even the usually detached atmosphere of the Supreme Court. In a 1970 cause célèbre concerning the question "Who is a Jew?" Justice Moshe Silberg wrote in a minority opinion: "We are a people dwelling alone and fighting alone. When our youthful fighters stood by themselves in battle facing a hostile world—at the best, indifferent—they saw clearly that *Israel has no friend but herself.*"[7]

"The nations of Europe who did not help us during the Holocaust," said Golda Meir in response to the growing criticism of her policies, "are not entitled to preach to us."[8] Later, this mood was reiterated and amplified by former Prime Minister Begin. Europe's anti-Israeli stand was directly linked by him to its long and bloody history of anti-Jewish persecution.

With the Yom Kippur War this period of self-righteousness and intoxication from imaginary power suffered a defeat. The vision of a solitary Israel defying the world could no longer be as attractive as it was during the days before October 1973. Israel's dependence on foreign aid grew to frightening proportions. Thus when Sadat's plane touched down at Ben Gurion Airport that Saturday night in November 1977, he found a country ready to trade Sinai, the very symbol of its conquests, for peace.

Yet, the suspicion of the outside world implanted during that period affected the national psyche. Its detrimental impact on the traditional, liberal, and humanitarian concepts of historical Zionism plus the fact that it was led and encouraged by Golda Meir's Labor Government is surely one of the paradoxes of that strange period. During that time only a few iconoclastic politicians and journalists asked where this mood might lead Israel and how it jibed with Zionism's aim to bring Israel into the community of nations.

Indeed the Yom Kippur War and the dramatic demonstration of Arab oil power, which followed it, worsened Israel's isolation. Third World countries, which had begun to sever their links with Israel before the war, completed the process after the war. Condemnation in the West grew to deafening dimensions. To Israelis, this was, and is, an unjust attitude, a cynical capitulation to Arab blackmail. Be that as it may, the country found itself a small Jewish island, menaced, misunderstood, and maligned by all, a successor to the Jewish community of older times. Like the old Jews, Israel now began to conceive of itself as fighting for survival in a foreign and alienated world which denies her rights accorded as a matter of routine to others. Many Israelis began to adopt a traditionally Jewish stance: There are the righteous few friends, such as Holland and much of the United States, just as there were such exceptional, righteous Gentiles in Jewish history; but the world is inherently a stranger—at best alienated, usually belligerent. Jewish fate, which Zionism sought to flee, had overtaken it. Of the song "The Whole World Is Against Us" only the refrain linking the grandsons "to our forefathers" remained relevant. The Yom Kippur War obliterated the part which told the world "to go to hell."

This post-Yom Kippur mood had a conflicting impact on the country. On the one hand, it induced Israel's gradual withdrawal from Sinai, which actually began in 1975 as a unilateral act with hardly a quid pro quo from the other side; on the other hand, Israel was asked to give up assets which almost all her citizens regard as vital to their very life. Hence, the despondency and the seeming paranoia. In this new ambience it was only natural that the small determined minority of religious-nationalist zealots—devoid of doubt, innocent of misgivings—would increase their hold over Israeli society. With the decline of traditional Zionist thought, with the fall of ideas of normalization, the irrational, messianic element grew stronger and manifested itself in every aspect of life: from mass demonstrations through the creation of illegal settlements to a rash of bumper stickers quoting Genesis, "Do not have fear, O my servant Jacob."

Indeed, Israelis swayed between two contradicting poles: the Zionist urge for normalization and the older Jewish instincts. Current moods reflect the relative strength of these two competing forces. When Israel's isolation grows, the influence of classic Jewish elements and their traditional reflexes surge to the surface, with the notion of a society encompassed by a hostile world taking root in a soil fed by generations-old subconscious fears. When "the world" sides with Israel in its few moments of glory, such as during the Six-Day War or the Entebbe rescue operation, the Zionist credo takes over.

As Arab power grew, Israel's position became more precarious. Arab propaganda, which even before 1967 had emphasized anti-Semitic sentiments, gained self-confidence and sophistication after the Six-Day War. Prompted by Arab propaganda and Third World rhetoric, a rabid stream of denunciation, culminating in the United Nations' "Zionism is racism" resolution was aimed against Israel. Israel itself—not her policies—was now being denounced from international pulpits as a "crime against humanity." Helped by their economic prowess, the Arabs unleashed against the Jewish state a campaign seeking to strip the country of its right to exist. The lyrics may have been new, but the tune was old and familiar to Jewish ears. Anti-Semitism, proscribed by an international consensus after the Holocaust, rose in the guise of anti-Zionism, directing its renascent wrath against the allegedly colonialist Israel. In the West, a new generation which never knew the Holocaust was willing to listen to these seemingly progressive views without detecting the oil-rich reactionary forces manipulating them.

Thus, the post–Six-Day War period ushered in not only a stronger affinity between Israel and the Diaspora—now perceived as the only true and constant ally—but also a new alliance between old and new foes of the Jews: the Arab states and the traditional Jew-baiting of the Russian East and the western Right. In the past, the Jews were told by the anti-Semites "to get out and go to Jerusalem;" now they were vilified for this very reason. The traditional European right—eager to appease the new Arab power—could, on this one issue, join hands with the New Left. For Soviet *agitprop*, nothing was more natural, more instinctive, than the combination of traditional, folk–anti-Semitism with a routine attack on Israel's "imperialistic, land-grabbing" policies. To their horror, the new Jews found themselves pilloried for the very same alleged faults as their forefathers'.

De Gaulle's lashing out against Israel after the Six-Day War—perhaps a politically insignificant event—exemplified this new situation: Before 1967, Charles de Gaulle personified

more than any other ruler Israel's new status. Israel was, according to his own phrase, "France's friend and ally." His
friendship to Israel, as well as the growing links with the
French Right, demonstrated the sharp distinction which the
French made, and the Israelis enjoyed, between Jews and Israelis. But after the war, when France's policy switched to a
pro-Arab stand, the French president shocked Israel by his reversal: he criticized Israel for the war, for refusing to withdraw,
and on November 27, 1967, denounced it as embodying all the
negative, traditional traits of the Jews, whom he defined as "an
elitist, arrogant and domineering people."

Israelis saw in this outburst a dramatic confirmation of a
doubt which had always lingered in their hearts: Despite the
provisional camouflage, the world, the goyim—including transient allies—remain anti-Jewish. De Gaulle's words proved
that Israel's existence did not cure this malady.

On the contrary, in its new exposed position it attracted new
forms and channels in which the old apparition could material-
ize anew. Israel was the inheritor of a parent she had always
rejected. De Gaulle's words provoked not only popular reactions but also some deeper reflections by academicians. Professor Baruch Kurzweill of Bar Ilan University wrote that de
Gaulle was the modern incarnation of the former Catholic
kings, whose homily was a direct "continuation of medieval
debates, couched in political-religious terms, which have been
going on for centuries between Christians and Jews."[9] Professor Saul Friedlander assumed that the latent anti-Semitism of
the Jesuit-educated president broke out because in his mind
Israel endangered French interests:

In order to camouflage cynical political considerations which may
have caused, if publicly acknowledged, certain resentment, the general found a metapolitical justification; an extreme anti-Israeli stand
can be more easily justified, if at the very core of Israel and the Zionist
movement lie aggressiveness and ambition which are the result of the
inherent qualities of the Jewish people.[10]

With the growth of the anti-Semitic slant in anti-Israeli propaganda, with the United Nations becoming the platform for a new brand of racism, Israelis reluctantly found themselves more and more playing the traditionally Jewish role of a scapegoat for humanity's ills. In the United Nations-inspired Conference on Women, which took place in Copenhagen in 1980, Israel—not hunger, not backwardness, not war—was blamed throughout the proceedings for every affliction, conceivable and inconceivable. Eliahu Salpeter, a columnist for *Ha'aretz* daily wrote: "Israel now is blamed, as the Jews of yesteryear, for Nature's disasters, as well as for the sufferings caused in underdeveloped societies through the greed and incompetence of their leaders."[11] The anti-Israeli offensive inspired in Israel a typically Jewish response.

Aharon Megged published in *Davar*, the Histadrut daily, a series of articles linking the predicament facing the Jewish state with traditional Jewish suffering. The libelous attacks against Israel were compared with the infamous blood libels against Jews for allegedly using Christian victims' blood for baking Passover matzoth. After the notorious Damascus blood libel of 1852 Ahad Ha'am wrote an article in which the libel was seen as a semi-consolation. Without such a preposterous accusation, Jews could have fallen into the trap of believing what the whole world had been saying about them: It is inconceivable that what so many different people have consistently been saying for so many years is utterly without foundation, a complete travesty, a bundle of lies; there must be at least some foundation for it. The blood libels enabled them to dismiss such doubts and apprehensions and to reassure themselves that the allegations were indeed all false. They could tell the world: You are all wrong and have been wrong all these generations. If you believe the blood libel, anything you may be saying against us is equally baseless.

Megged used the same reasoning for the United Nations' vehement diatribe against the Jewish state: When Zionism is decried as racism—by nations whose whole structure is founded upon racial exclusiveness—then Israelis, in the wake of their ancestors, can say: Everything which you ever said about us is equally false. This conflict, argued Megged, is not new:

The all-seeing satellite encircling the globe aims its telescopic camera at one tiny spot on the shores of the Mediterranean, photographs it and blows up the picture ten thousandfold: This is the enemy! The enemy of humanity!. . . This disproportion which distorts the face of the world to the point of a caricature in which the Jewish nose is the focal point—is a fact. . . . This phenomenon does not fall into the category of "every nation is a wolf to the other." No, this is a "special case," one and only in the annals of history, one and only even in this age of progress.[12]

If these words sound familiar—an echo of Nordau's famous address to the First Zionist Congress—it is no accident. This is indeed the echo of the disappointment and frustration which was the lot of the Jews one hundred years before, toward the end of the nineteenth century, when emancipated and progressive Jews were watching with helpless stupefaction the volcanic eruption of an anti-Semitism long considered dead. Israelis began saying to themselves that they were witnessing an irrational, but tragically consistent, phenomenon: The refusal of the Christian West to accept assimilation and the refusal of the Arab-Moslem world to accept a Jewish national presence in the Middle East was followed by the world's refusal to accept Israel—an Israel which seeks to be a normal member of the world community.

More significant was the failure of the Israelis—at least the secular Israelis—to understand the reason for this new eruption of the old volcano. In this respect, too, Israelis shared their lot with nineteenth-century emancipated Jews and were unlike their religious ancestors who could endure traditional anti-Semitism.

Medieval anti-Semitism was intolerable and unrelenting in its oppression of the defenseless Jewish minority. But it contained some guarantees for Jews and had a theological raison d'être. Although the Jews could not accept their image as the killers of Christ, the reasoning did contain a logic of its own. The Jews were the keepers of the Covenant and their sufferings were part of a collision between two faiths. The purpose of Christian anti-Semitism was twofold: the censure and punishment of the Jews and the constant striving to lead them into the Mother Church, thereby demonstrating her rightness. Thus it was necessary for theological reasons to keep the Jews alive. The intention was to oppress and persecute them, but not to destroy them. The Jews were to be witnesses to the truth of the New Testament, and survive as a living exemplar, as a people dispersed among the nations, in punishment for their sins.

The assimilation and emancipation of the nineteenth century were supposed to put an end to such superstition and prejudice. But the utterly bewildered modern Jews discovered that these had been supplanted by a new monster; for the first time they encountered a secular and racial anti-Semitism, lacking any religious inhibitions or indeed any rationale, theological or otherwise. Religious Judaism could cope, albeit with dreadful suffering, with the Inquisition, persecution and pogroms, overcoming through martyrdom their torturers. Their deaths had a religious significance; it was the Sanctification of God's Name, *Kiddush Hashem*. Belief clashed with belief, religion with religion, Messiah with Messiah. The historical combinations of Jew pitted against Christian could somehow coexist: Nachmanides and Pablo Cristiani; Pope Benedictus XIII and Rabbi Joseph Albo; Nicholas Donin and Rabbi Yehiel of Paris. Each side found a meaning and justification in this confrontation—if one may use such an expression for the persecution of the weak by the strong.

The new twins—secular Judaism and modern anti-Semitism—which arose like the phoenix from the ashes of the Dark Ages, could not coexist. Zionism was, therefore, the only solution. Yet a hundred years later, Israelis found themselves in the same perplexed position. Irrational reality clashed with their very philosophy.

The secular Israelis could not cope with the new animosity, just as Dr. Herzl could not cope with the anti-Dreyfus mob in Paris. Harvard professor Nathan Glazer wrote in the wake of the Yom Kippur War:

Jews for the most part have wanted to be like everybody else. Indeed, ironically, the establishment of Israel was an attempt to make Jews like everybody else. They would now have a state. It has not worked out that way. Israel has made Jews more, not less, exceptional. The pariah people, it seems, have simply succeeded in creating a pariah state.[13]

This awareness has radically altered Israel's mood. The inter-relationship with the outside world is not a side issue but the one subject on which different Zionist factions agreed. It is this factor which explains the meteoric rise and disproportionate power exercised by the religious-nationalist zealots: They had all the answers to Israel's problems. By relating all her difficulties to the old conflict between Jews and Gentiles, they could furnish a consistent, historical answer to the mystifying riddle. It is no accident, therefore, that the post–1967 period saw a double shift of power. The right-of-center Likud unseated the Labor party which, in the face of the growing hostility to Israel, lost much that distinguished it in the past from the Right; within the Right, the new religious leaders inherited the place occupied in the past by Jabotinsky's Revisionist party. Gush Emunim, leading this new nationalist wave, forced its will upon successive wavering cabinets. In a period of confusion and bewilderment, they represented conviction and commitment.

In fact, a deeper process was taking place. Zionism sought to escape the exilic experience, and now galut was forcefully returning, uninvited, to the house which Zionism built. From this point of view, De Gaulle, on the one hand, and Golda Meir and Menachem Begin, on the other, complement each other. Begin made an analogy between the European persecution of the Jews and its policy toward Israel; De Gaulle made an analogy between Jewish behavior—as seen through his Catholic eyes—and Israel's foreign policy. The circle was completed on both sides: It really does not matter that the Jews had a just grievance and that claims such as those made by De Gaulle were without any foundation. And the circle is completed in that galut returned to Israel with all its layers, including the sense of the injustice perpetrated against the Jews.

The change in Israel's direction after the 1967 war was dramatic and apparently sudden. However, this change could not have taken place without the prior preparation. The roots of the new era lay underground, providing the collective psyche of Israelis with new food for thought.

The two central events that brought about Israel's birth were the Holocaust and the War of Independence. The experience of newly won sovereignty was so overwhelming that it pushed from national awareness the full meaning of the Holocaust. But as time passed and the veil of secrecy was lifted from classified documents, the West's betrayal of Europe's Jews and a new recognition of Jewish aloneness became painfully apparent. In 1961 Eichmann stood trial in Jerusalem, and young Israelis heard for the first time the full tale of the horror which had occurred just a few years before statehood. That transition between the most tragic demonstration of Jewish helplessness and the rebirth of Jewish power—between doom and dawn—was so sharp, so traumatic that its full impact filtered only gradually into the consciousness of the nation. Just a few years separated the total subjugation of Jews to the Nazi murder machine from their heroic victories in Palestine. Within a short span of time, those orphans of Auschwitz, the relics of Europe's Jewry, became fighter pilots and tank commanders. Within the very same generation, the Jew was transformed from victim to victor. In Amos Oz's unforgettable novel, *A Late Love*, the elderly hero daydreams about an Israeli armored column marching through Europe avenging the blood of the innocents:

And with lightning speed my tanks turn and thunder eastward. It's coming, it's coming, it's here. With furious wrath they hound all the bands of the butchers of the Jews: Poles, Lithuanians, Ukrainians. . . . And I see Moshe Dayan, in his dusty battle dress, standing awesome and gaunt, as he receives in a grim silence the surrender of the governor general of Kishinev.[14]

But the reflections on this contrast between the stooped march to the gas chambers and the march of Israel's armed heroes raised anew the question of the alleged inherent difference between the galut Jews and the new Hebrews. Was this metamorphosis solely a product of the new reality, of the Zionist rebirth? Is the galut Jew's inferiority truly inherent? And can anti-Semitism be remedied by the Zionist cure-all?

Chief of Staff General David "Daddo" Elazar addressed this question a short time before the outbreak of the Yom Kippur War, in a ceremony commemorating the thirtieth anniversary of the Warsaw Ghetto uprising:

Only five years separate 1943 from 1948, between the revolt of the ghettoes, and the battles of liberation in our land. Only five years separate the most horrific tragedy that our people have ever known from their most glorious victory. When we, fighters of the Palmach, first heard on the sandy beaches of Caesaria the tale told us by the survivors of the Warsaw Ghetto, we felt that we belonged to the same fighting corps, sons of the same nation, fighting the same war. We do not know why and for what reason those millions were massacred in the days of that total eclipse. We do know that they died a thousand cruel and unusual deaths because they were the exiles, the different, the weak, and because we did not have the State of Israel in those cruel days. This is why we are convinced that power is vital. This is why we have sworn to be strong and well armed. This is why we have decided not to live by the sufferance of others.[15]

Such expressions began to raise doubts about truisms previously taken for granted. The Sabra fighter was not inherently different from his allegedly inferior step-brothers. No fault lay with them save their otherness. Their betrayal by the outside world, during World War II, aroused new doubts as to the authenticity of the acceptance of the Jewish state after the war. Did the United Nations General Assembly vote for the partition of Palestine, on that historic night of November 29, 1947, really signify the opening of a new chapter in the relationship between Jews and Gentiles? Was the recognition of Israel truly a revolutionary occurrence which would have long-range effects, or was it merely a passing event, a nervous and short-lived reaction to European and Christian guilt? Are not the lessons of the Holocaust doomed to be forgotten as the unbearable sights fade into oblivion?

Saul Friedlander, himself a survivor from Nazi Europe, attempted to grapple with these lingering doubts. He dealt with the analogy made by Hannah Arendt between the pariah Jew and the hero of Franz Kafka's *The Castle*, who cannot gain admittance to the castle because he is the foreigner, the non-belonger. Friedlander saw the analogy particularly pertinent with regard to the end of the novel. When the outsider, the pariah Jew, believes that he is invited to enter the etablishment represented by the castle, he discovers that no one is really ready to accept him. He then becomes a half-hearted revolutionary, rebelling against this palpable injustice, siding with the other outcasts of the social system. But the real end of *The Castle*—which Kafka never wrote but which he related to his friend Max Brod—is the most poignant. The hero, the pariah, sinks lower and lower into an abject state, when suddenly a message arrives from the castle: He is accepted. But the message comes too late, the hero is dying or is already dead. Comments Friedlander:

When, at the end of the war, western society opened its arms to the Jews; when, in reaction to the discovery of the whole magnitude of the Nazi massacres, the western anti-Semitic tradition was—temporarily at least—discarded, most of the Jews of Europe could no longer enter into that new society. But the most terrible question remains to be answered, the one question that will probably never find its answer, although for us it is the most crucial one to understand the past or foresee events to come: Did the castle send the messenger because the injustice, the evil done, was recognized? Or was the messenger sent because the hero was dead?[16]

These are not easily said words and they are voiced by a spokesman for reason and moderation within Israel. But if such doubts can be cast about the reconciliation between Jews and non-Jews in the wake of Israel's independence, how can one support the basic tenets of Zionist ideology? Had not Herzl been oblivious to the irrational and, therefore, ineradicable element in the rejection of the Jews by the outside world? Is not Herzlian Zionism guilty of a naïve belief which turns a blind eye to an ancient and even pre-Christian phenomenon?

Had Israel lived in peace with its Middle Eastern neighbors, it would have been possible to discuss these probing questions dispassionately and frame them within the appropriate global and historical perspectives. But Israel was fated, from its inception, to experience war and Arab rejection, which forged a link between Israelis and their galut parents. In the years preceding the 1967 war, such moods did not pervade the mainstream of Israeli thinking, but their latent rumblings could be heard by the trained ear. Still heading the state in those years were the founding fathers for whom Israel continued to be a miracle, to be anxiously guarded by incorporating her into the fabric of international society. These leaders still clung to the Herzlian credo and staunchly believed in Israel's socialist message.

By the time the Six-Day War broke out, that message had already been eroded by the constant abrasion of harsh facts. From the days of fervor, of pioneering communes and utopian visions, Labor Zionism had to move to a position of political and economic leadership in a country beset by increasingly painful problems. Originally Labor had seen itself as a future leader of the world, as a potential redeemer of the Arab working classes. Through the communal settlements, the Histadrut and the cooperative movement, Labor sought to provide a universal example to both the advanced industrial societies and the underdeveloped countries. Many of Labor's unique achievements have survived the transition from Yishuv to state. Its system of productive cooperation from the urban cooperative through the partially private moshav to the total collectivity of a kibbutz remains, to this day, the only viable and long-lasting example of a voluntary and successful escape from the lure of private property and individual gain. The Histadrut, with its vast network of social and educational work and its own blooming industrial enterprises, is still a singular example defying the traditional line dividing employers and employees. The kibbutz movement has seen the rise and fall of various fashionable commune movements while it adapted to changing circumstances by moving from an exclusively agrarian existence to sophisticated industry. But despite all these truly magnificent achievements, Labor has not succeeded in carrying out Ben Gurion's much-touted slogan of Israel becoming *am segula*, a "chosen" or model nation. Its own socialist tenets have been frustrated by a new post-state reality. Independence has brought to Israel's teeming shores the tired, the poor refugees from Arab and Moslem countries. They have come from underprivileged and undereducated societies, and for them the transition from religious-patriarchal patterns to the secular socialist values of the old-time European settlers has been too radical a step. Most of the new immigrants have bypassed the kibbutz movement and gradually formed a new proletariat, whose special problems did not fit into Labor's traditional organization and program. On the international front, Labor managed to establish good relations with her sister-parties abroad, had a good standing in the Socialist International, and became a focal point of interest and education for African and Asian students, politicians, and labor leaders. But the voice of its universal message was lost in the sound and fury of the Arab-Jewish wars. In the fifties, the Soviet-led bloc, the "world of the future," for whom Labor Zionism had a traditional affinity, and with whom leftist factions had fleeting love affairs, turned from friend to foe. In the sixties, the New Left picked Israel as an appropriate target for hate and derision and, together with South Africa, the Jewish state was branded an outcast. Israel, which had set out to lead the world into a new epoch of justice and equality, found itself, even before 1967,

gradually edged out of the new Third World entente in which
the Moslem and Arab states have played a leading role. The
potential leader of enslaved workers was now being castigated
as the alleged last stronghold of white imperialism in Asia.

After the Herzlian disappointment with European liberalism
at the turn of the century, after the treachery of Europe's extreme Right during World War II, came growing disenchantment with the Left. In the post-World War I era, Zionism was
fashionable in progressive circles because it fell within the
accepted matrix of self-determination. But after World War II,
this concept was conceived as applicable only to the nonwhite,
non-European world. Israel was perceived as falling outside
this category despite its non-European majority and its socialist message was often rejected because of this alleged blemish.
On the domestic front, too, Labor lost after statehood much of
its former appeal. The utopian message was gradually crushed
by the necessity to accommodate Israel's conflicting needs.
Industrialization required a new capitalist approach which was
hardly compatible with the Tolstoyan ideals of a return to the
soil. Agriculture could not absorb the massive waves of new
Jewish refugees; nor was it capable, because of the scarcity of
water and land, to solve the country's economic problems. In
the communal settlements, the traditional commandment of
self-work was tainted by the growing employment of hired
labor—usually Arab daily workers. A prolonged and unchallenged labor rule proved the universality of Lord Acton's famous dictum about power which corrupts.

The messianic fervor, the semireligious zeal, which was the
hallmark of the pioneering days, as well as the belief that Israel
would "redeem the world which crucified him," gradually
dwindled and eventually vanished. The attempt to clothe the
old Jewish idea of chosenness in a modern mantle of progress
ended in abject failure. Parallel to this decline of socialist belief, a resurgence of religious feelings gradually emerged. This
change did not manifest itself in an increase in religious obser-

vance. On the contrary, despite the mass immigration from Islamic countries which brought in a large observant community, and despite the higher birth rate of the religious families, the proportion between secular and observant Israelis has remained constant since the early days of 1948. One indicator attesting to this surprising stability is the representation of the religious parties, which in ten successive Knessets has oscillated between 10 and 14 percent. The drift toward religion took place within the secular majority and was expressed not by a revival of faith but by a growing skepticism regarding the secular Zionist denial of the viability and durability of the religious tradition. Thus, while not turning to religion, many Israelis began to harbor a disbelief in the power of the new Jewish nationalism to replace traditional Jewish values. Moreover, the negation of the galut, the total rejection of Diaspora existence, went hand in hand with the denial of Jewish history in exile. In a post-Holocaust world, the attitude toward the destroyed Jewish communities of Europe underwent a metamorphosis. Instead of the previous rejection, a new sense of loss and nostalgia enveloped Israeli Jews. The despised Yiddish—the former "enemy language"—became the ember remaining from the great fire, a testimony of a world worthy of preservation and love but gone with the flames. The millions who died in Nazi Europe were Yiddish-speaking Jews, and Israelis began to feel that they must not betray the memory of the dead by turning their backs on everything they represented. The Yishuv's term "Hebrew" gradually disappeared and "Jew" returned as a common usage. The Yishuv and its institutions were all Hebrew, never Jewish. Israel forsook this terminology and perceived itself as Jewish. In the twenties and thirties "Jew" had a pejorative meaning. In post-Holocaust Israel, the law does not allow an Israeli to define his ethnic membership as Hebrew. The Jewish shtetl, formerly the embodiment of everything inferior and derogatory, acquired a new aura: It was seen as the miraculous island of civilization in a sea of ignorance and hatred. A revival of shtetl culture and literature began, and many of its former vices were now depicted as virtues.

This new mood began to cast doubt on the capacity of the Jews to discard their Jewish past and to throw off their hereditary mantle. Zionism had sought to create a complete metamorphosis, to evolve a Hebrew butterfly from the Jewish cocoon, to send into current history an independent Zionist state separated from the diaspora; but that endeavor succeeded only partially. The new Hebrew found himself—regardless of his intentions—intertwined with his roots, and ancestry was seen not as relating to distant biblical times but to father's burntout home.

Nowhere is this change more apparent than within the Labor movement. The attitude to Jewish tradition changes from alienation to an urgent wish to preserve its treasures. The socialist fathers were rebels, but they knew the tradition against which they rebelled. Their Israeli sons were given a totally secular education, and consequently the elderly ex-revolutionaries were now beginning to be afraid lest the very knowledge of Judaism die with them. It was a Labor minister of education, Zalman Aran, who, in the late fifties, took the unprecedented step of introducing "Jewish consciousness" studies into the state secular school curriculum. Within the kibbutz movement a reassessment of Jewish values took place. The translation of Jewish holidays into a new secular-socialist language was halted and suffered defeat. In many kibbutzim, a search for Jewish roots began: Parts of the traditional Passover Haggadah were restored to the Seder ceremonies. It was occasionally even permissible to regard Yom Kippur as a holy day of fast and repentance. The kibbutz synagogue, originally built as an anachronistic reserve for observant parents of members, began to receive new visitors—some coming for a curious look at the strange, distant and yet close world, others regularly attending that remnant of a lost past. A re-examination of the Zionist-socialist gospel became an essential part of kibbutz literature and journalism. Aharon Megged, a spokesman for this soul searching, articulated the new skepticism on the pages of *Davar*, the Histadrut daily:

We are slowly and gradually turning back. And if this process is to be continued and accelerated, we shall soon return to pre-emancipation days. Every vacuum—as we have learned—must fill up. Gone is the socialist religion of work and its place is being taken by our father's religion. Is this so bad? Is this worse than total emptiness?[17]

It was this disillusionment with socialism, this new sense of emptiness and fear of hollowness, which lay the groundwork for the post-1967 rise of militant religious nationalism. Labor's ideological fortress, even before that watershed event, lay in ruins and when the challenge came, there were few guards ready to man its crumbling ramparts.

This decline of a formerly omnipotent ideology is best demonstrated by an incident which occurred in 1976, when the northern border with the Christian enclaves of Southern Lebanon was opened, and through the "Good Fence" new contacts were made with Lebanese villagers. Israeli television was at hand to cover the dramatic meeting between Jews and Arabs across the barbed-wire barrier which had separated them since 1948. Among the Lebanese villagers were a few who remembered the pre-state days, and some even spoke a little Hebrew. The star attraction was a woman who spoke fluent Hebrew, having attended one of the camps which the Labor movement organized before 1948 in order to promote Arab-Jewish understanding. She remembered a song from those olden days, one of the hymns of the Labor movement, and sang it before the television cameras:

> *Flame! Go up, flame*
> *We shall labor with the hammer all the long day*
> *Flame! Go up, flame!*
> *Like You, our flag is red, red all over.*

As the Lebanese woman finished singing, a deep embarrassed silence descended on her Israeli entourage and on the television viewers. In post-state Israel, no one was singing these outdated lines any more. Little remained but half-hearted lip service to socialism. The ground was prepared for a new political passion.

7

THE NEW RELIGIOUS MILITANCY

ON April 4, 1968, the eve of Passover, a group of sixty Israeli Jews arrived at Hebron. With their children, the ten families went to a small Arab hotel which they had rented for the holidays. The members of the group had told the Israeli military authorities that they were going to stay in the hotel for only two days; to the owner of the hotel, they presented themselves as tourists from Switzerland. Ostensibly, no fault could be found with this pilgrimage of observant Jews seeking to spend the Holidays in a town whose very name arouses biblical memories.

Yet, this innocuous Passover in Hebron marked the rise of a new religious movement destined to change the course of Israel's fortunes.

The ten families were headed by Rabbi Moshe Levinger, up to then a marginal figure known in religious circles for his total devotion, as well as for his quarrelsome nature. Under his leadership, the mission to Hebron was well organized: the families were all hand picked; the financing was done by the Movement for Greater Israel which originated after 1967; the whole operation was kept secret from mass media and came as a total surprise to most cabinet members.

The visitors took over the two-story Park Hotel, turned its kitchen kosher, celebrated the Seder in high spirits, and went on to announce that they were not going to let anyone eject them from the town of the Patriarchs.

The cabinet was caught unaware by this unilateral act. Levinger's men were openly defying the government's authority, blatantly trying to force its hand and compel it to include Hebron in its settlement plans. The military authorities and the defense establishment were patently resentful. Hebron, a devout Moslem town, had not been giving the Israelis any trouble at the time and its mayor, Sheikh Ali Ja'abri, cooperated with the military authorities in ensuring a peaceful coexistence between the Hebronites and the new regime. It was no accident that no representative of the military governor came to visit the Jewish guests exposed to danger in midst of an Arab town. But others did come: rabbis, settlers from nearby kibbutzim, leaders of the Movement for Greater Israel and hundreds of enthusiastic supporters from all over the country. The news that the Jews were returning to Hebron ignited a dormant spark of half-forgotten memories. Hebron was the town where the patriarch Abraham, the Father of the Nation, bought for four hundred shekels of silver his first piece of land in Canaan, the field of Ephron the Hittite. In the Cave of Machpelah he buried his wife Sarah, thus gaining the first foothold in a land promised to his seed.

For hundreds of years, after the Jews went into Exile, Hebron remained with Jerusalem, Safed, and Tiberias, one of the "holy cities," in which the scattered Jewish communities in Palestine huddled, waiting for Redemption. In 1929, its thriving Jewish community was virtually wiped out by an Arab massacre and the tales of the atrocities committed then became imprinted in the national memory of the Yishuv. After the 1929 riots, Jews were not permitted to live in Hebron. Since the Moslem Conquest of Palestine, Jews were not allowed to enter the Tomb of the Patriarchs, a mosque which the Moslems regarded as exclusively theirs. It was time to right this humiliating wrong. Labor Minister Yigal Allon, who also came to visit Rabbi Levinger's group in order to lend support, said: "There have always been Jews in Hebron, the cradle of the nation, until they were violently uprooted. . . . It is inconceivable that Jews be prohibited from settling in this ancient town of the Patriarchs."[1]

Thus began a protracted cat-and-mouse game between a hesitant and divided government and a determined, widely supported group. The religious settlers had not only faith on their side; they also spoke in the name of the very right upon which the Zionist claim to Eretz Israel has always been founded.

The settlers' announcement that they were not going to leave Hebron, prompted a nationwide debate. Emotion clashed with reason. Thinking Israelis foresaw the dangers which the resettlement of Hebron harbored and *Ha'aretz*, the Tel Aviv daily, warned against succumbing to this fait accompli. Theirs was a reasoned appeal to accept the partition of Palestine between Jews and Arabs and to refrain from actions which would both disrupt the peaceful relations with the Hebronites and weaken Israel's international posture. But these arguments seemed ineffective in the face of such highly charged symbols as the settlers' wish to celebrate the return to Hebron of a Torah scroll saved from the 1929 pogrom. The Torah had been saved from the blazing synagogue by a rabbi who later died from burns suffered in the rescue, the scroll at his head. Before he died, the rabbi bequeathed the scroll to a friend, stipulating that when the Jews returned to Hebron, he should bring the Torah back to its ancient abode. Now the grandson of that venerable rabbi was seeking to fulfill his last will and testament. Could this wish be denied by the Jewish authorities? Could reasons of expedience countervail such an act of faith? Indeed, the military authorities eventually had to rescind their prohibition against the public installation of the scroll at the settlers' newly established synagogue, even though such action lent an air of permanence to what started as a pilgrimage.

Under the tutelage of the religious parties, the rabbinical establishment, and elements within Labor, Rabbi Levinger's group began to take root. By the end of May, they were moved into the military governor's compound, where they kept charging the government with seeking to isolate the group and bring about its gradual attrition. When they disobeyed the military orders regarding their behavior at the Tomb of the Patriarchs, five settlers were ordered to leave Hebron. This created a political storm, which Levi Eshkol's split government could not weather. Under pressure, Defense Minister Moshe Dayan had to annul the order. The pattern was thus set: The settlers create "facts"; the government responds half-heartedly, with some of its ministers openly supporting the settlers; the government reaches a compromise; the settlers create another "fact."

Eventually, the cabinet had to accept the settlers' intent to stay in Hebron. In August 1968, they were allowed to open a yeshiva, limiting the number of its members to one hundred and three. In the Tomb of the Patriarchs, within the Mosque of Abraham, the settlers were gradually getting more space and more time for Jewish prayers in a building which for hundreds of years had been exclusively Moslem.

The Moslem leaders protested, time and time again, against what they regarded as Jewish encroachment of their ancient rights. The settlers insisted on their right to pray according to their own practice, occasionally disregarding Moslem prayer hours. To the settlers, the Tomb was not only a Moslem mosque; it was the burial site which the Book of Genesis speaks of with such loving detail.

Tension in Arab Hebron was rising rapidly—the Tomb of the Patriarchs constituting one of the principal causes. In September 1968, after the Jewish New Year services extended beyond the agreed time limit, the dignitaries and religious sages of Hebron issued a protest saying that "the prayers of the Jews in our sacred Mosque are a wound in the hearts of all believers throughout the world of Islam."[2] On October 9, the second day of Succot, a short time after this protest was made, a hand grenade was thrown into a crowd of hundreds of Israelis waiting to get into the Tomb. On the steps leading to the Mosque— where before 1967 Jews were not allowed to proceed beyond the seventh step—wounded, bleeding, screaming men, women, and children lay on the ground. Forty-seven were seriously wounded, among them a two-month-old baby. The shattering photos appeared next day on the front page, while in the back pages editorials clamored for governmental "response" to the atrocity. The response came within days. The cabinet decided to build a Jewish town overlooking Hebron. Kiryat Arba—the biblical twin name for Hebron—was established. It is now a city of over three thousand inhabitants, a symbol of religious-nationalist tenacity, a precedent for similar "facts," a source of pride, of regret, and of controversy to Israelis.

Rabbi Levinger's enterprise demonstrated the new orientation of religious Jewry, as well as its newly discovered power. Kiryat Arba indicated that the religious-nationalist movement now had the determination, the stamina, and the men to impose its will upon a wavering political establishment.

The new self-confidence gave birth to Gush Emunim. The Gush officially came into being in 1974, shortly after the Yom Kippur War. But Gush members were active as a pro-settlement movement from the successful enterprise of Kiryat Arba. The group consisted of idealistic young men and women within the National Religious Party circles and was naturally embraced by the Greater Israel Movement. They were educated in state religious schools and Bnai Akiva, a religious youth movement whose graduates set up some of the country's most successful communal settlements. Many of the Gush leaders went to a yeshiva headed by Rabbi Zvi Yehuda Kook, son of Chief Rabbi Kook, who in an earlier generation had established the doctrinal bridge linking religious and secular Zionists. Before the war, their voice had never been heard in political controversies. They were, up to then, the "knitted skullcap good boys"—a reference to the one article of clothing and their unassuming manners that distinguished them from their secular Sabra contemporaries. But after the "liberation of our forefathers' estate" in Hebron they were to become the religious spearhead of a national demand to retain the whole of Eretz Israel under Jewish sovereignty and to implement this claim by settlement.

When dealing with the phenomenon of Gush Emunim and

other groups of religious-nationalist zealotry which sprang into
action after 1967, it is important to realize that their significance is not confined to the political arena and does not lie
merely in their ability to force their will upon the country.
Gush Emunim—the name is used here collectively to denote
all the religious militant groups—provides a vociferous, and
occasionally, theatrical voice to a wider tendency within Israeli society. Just as the Hebrew "Canaanites" were in effect an
expression of the Yishuv education which saw in the negation
of galut the essence of the new society, so the dedicated members of the Gush are a product of post-state society and the
state religious education network. In the Yishuv there were
also religious personalities who saw in the Return to Eretz
Israel and its settlement the beginning of redemption in the
religious sense, but never before were the deeds and actions
themselves clothed with a messianic meaning. In addition, religious Zionists shared with their secular colleagues a philosophy which saw Jewish nationalism in a universal and humanistic context. The two main religious parties, Hamizrachi and
Ha'poel Hamizrachi, never resorted to mystical terms and
never cast any doubt on the underlying Herzlian premises of
Zionist thought. On the contrary, in the period preceding the
Six-Day War, the religious parties, who sat in a Labor-led government coalition, were the traditional spokesmen for moderation and restraint in the country's foreign and defense policy
and often spoke out and voted against the retaliatory border
raids which Ben Gurion initiated in the 1950s.

The new religious tenor of the post-1967 mood was radically
different and viewed the whole Zionist endeavor in a new
light. Rabbi Yehuda Amital, head of a Gush yeshiva, defined
this Zionism of Redemption:

This Zionism does not seek to solve the problem of the Jews by
setting up a Jewish state but is an instrument in the hands of the
Almighty which prepares the people of Israel for their Redemption.
The settlement of Eretz Israel through the ingathering of her sons, the

greening of her deserts, and the establishment of Jewish independence within it are merely stages in this process of Redemption. The purpose of this process is not the normalization of the people of Israel—to be a nation like all other nations—but to be a holy people, a people of a living God.[3]

This open defiance of Herzlian Zionism—and of everything the Labor movement stood for—was repeated wherever and whenever the Gush spokesmen defined their philosophy. Their views are characterized by a self-confidence untarnished by any doubt or uncertainty. The Six-Day War and the Yom Kippur War brought in their wake typical, soul-searching dialogues among secular Sabra soldiers. Some of these dialogues were published and were acclaimed for their inherent humanity, hatred of war, yearning for peace. But a similar dialogue at a Gush yeshiva, yielded no self-doubt. The specter of constant war and bloodshed did not deter the participants. Rabbi Meir Yehiel rejected the very ideas which have become synonymous with Zionism: "We have not settled here to look for peace and quiet; we have come here despite the sound and the fury, in order to fulfill the Lord's command; consequently, no obstacle shall obstruct or hinder us."[4]

This was the state of mind of the Gush and its many supporters. Their credo was enchantingly simple: the Land of Israel to the People of Israel according to the Torah of Israel. The existence of a prosperous Diaspora did not weaken their resolve because a true fulfillment of religious commandments—principally, the commandment to settle the land of Israel—was truly possible only in Israel. Chosenness needs no substitute because it relates directly to the idea of the Covenant between God and His people as manifested in the new reality of Israel. Israel is the embodiment of that Covenant.

Israel's difficulties may thus be explained in the light of its ancient history and special mission. Biblical quotes acquire a direct relevance, and its wars and armed struggles are an integral part of a truly messianic process leading to true Redemption.

The Lord's words to Abraham acquire, in the eyes of the Gush followers, a direct, political meaning. The land is bestowed by Divine Will whose authority cannot be gainsaid by secular institutions and considerations of political expedience. The recruits of the Gush are Israelis, molded in the state religious school network (which is financed by public funds but has its own independent supervisory boards and curricula). Unlike the Zionist religious founders who were educated in Europe and were constantly aware of the precarious situation of the Jews, these young militants grew up in an atmosphere emphasizing Israel's might and the world's hostility. More important is the Gush readiness to apply the traditional pioneering spirit to the new reality: They call on their faithful to leave towns, abandon their comfortable urban abodes, and settle the barren land—in the tradition of the old days of unadulterated idealism. The Bible lives in the ancient names they give their settlements, in the constant reference to the sights and sounds linking the new Jewish presence to evidence of its past glory: the Tomb of the Patriarchs in Hebron, the wall built by King Herod around Solomon's Temple, the very hills—Shiloh and Beth-El—where Jewish kings and priests uttered their immortal words.

After the victory in Hebron the Gush succeeded not only within the religious segment, transforming it from a moderate force to the vanguard of extremism, but also within large parts of the secular sector. Many nonobservant Israelis, including major political and literary figures, began to regard the Gush as the true executors of a national will, as the authentic successors to the pioneering tradition and a valuable barrier to compromise with, and surrender to, external pressures. Within Labor itself a circle was formed which pledged allegiance to the Gush, and its policy found favor in Labor's settlement lobby. The influence of the Gush—always numerically a small fractional minority—upon Labor cannot be overestimated. They imposed their will upon successive Labor cabinets and forced the government's hand on critical issues. They openly defied

Rabin's cabinet by establishing in 1973 an illegal settlement in Sebastia, threatened to clash with the army and managed, despite this challenge to the government's authority, to have their way.

In reality they did not have to force their will; the Labor cabinets themselves were split on the proper attitude to the Gush, and many of their tacit supporters occupied important positions in Labor's hierarchy. In the crucial period between 1974 and 1977, when Labor lost its plurality, there were three competing Labor leaders vying for hegemony: Prime Minister Rabin, Defense Minister Shimon Peres, and Foreign Minister Yigal Allon. Each had his own Gush supporter within his ministry: Rabin employed General Ariel Sharon as a special adviser; Peres had Yuval Ne'eman, who became a leader of the extremist pro-Gush *Hatechiyah* (Renaissance) party, directing Gush operations openly from the defense ministry; and Allon was the patron of Rabbi Levinger of Kiryat Arba fame. This was not a coincidence but a demonstration of Gush power over a long-divided Labor house.

When the Likud came into power in 1977, the hold of the Gush over the government was complete. Prime Minister Begin had been an avid Gush supporter before his ascent to power when he participated in their marches and attended the ceremonies establishing their settlements. Under his leadership, the government elevated the Gush to a leading settlement movement; showered money on its projects, creating in effect a Gush militia in their settlements; and surrendered to its wishes whenever there was a clash of wills. The Camp David accords and the peace treaty with Egypt hindered this romance with the government, but on the Gush major point, the settlement of Judea and Samaria, the two agreed. Any government attempts to resist the growing demands of the Gush gave way to their "moral pressure." The establishment of Elon Moreh is an example.

At the beginning of 1979, the Gush wanted to settle on a hilltop overlooking Nablus in a location with no viable future and which many experts—including the then defense minister, Ezer Weizman—dismissed as having no security value. The government opposed the idea but capitulated after a series of tenacious demonstrations and sit-ins by devout Gush families, and decided to confiscate private Arab land in order to put up Elon Moreh, the biblical name for the site where Abraham built an altar to the Lord after His promise to give the land of Canaan to his seed. In the ensuing legal battle, Gush lawyers admitted in the Supreme Court that they were not motivated by security but by their mission derived from their Judaic belief. The Court, relying partially on the arguments of the Gush itself, ruled that private land could be confiscated only on grounds of military necessity and ordered the evacuation of the settlement. A war of nerves ensued. The settlers threatened to disobey the Court's ruling and to defy the government's orders. After much delay, they agreed to heed to the law only upon condition that a nearby alternative location be given to Elon Moreh. The government agreed and the army's assistance was enlisted to make the settlement ready in accordance with Gush diktat.

From such incidents, both the growing power of the new religious militancy and the weakness of the wavering majority as represented by a democratically elected government are apparent. It was hardly a question of the Gush imposing its will upon reluctant cabinets. As in the precedent-setting case of Kiryat Arba, it was rather the case of a half-hearted refusal by Labor and Likud governments which led to a willing submission.

In Begin's second term, starting in 1981—as well as under Shamir's cabinet—there was no need to resort to such tactics. Settlement on a wide scale on expropriated land acquired new dimensions with the establishment of "dormitory suburbs" in the West Bank, thus luring many Israelis to purchase an apartment or a house, attractively priced, within an easy ride from their work. Gush Emunim can be seen as the ideological trailblazers in whose steps followed thousands of ordinary Israelis.

Thus after the 1967 watershed, the Gush became the spearhead, the guiding light, of the new Israeli Right. This new Right has three components: the Labor supporters of the Movement for Greater Israel; the new religious zealots; and the old nationalist Right, formerly the Jabotinsky-led Revisionists, now transformed into the Begin-led Herut party. The Gush transformed the old Revisionist Right. The new Right was hardly recognizable as the heir of the old nationalists.

Young Israelis find it hard to believe that Begin's forerunners were wholly irreligious and objected to any form of religious tampering with politics. Jabotinsky—Begin's leader and mentor—was so detached from ways Judaic that he advocated the adoption of Latin script for modern Hebrew and willed his body to be cremated—an act that is contrary to Jewish law and every Jewish instinct. Today, it is difficult to believe that the atheist Nordau, the total European who was ready to forego the Jewish Sabbath, was acclaimed by the old Revisionists as their very own prophet and his writings were published by them. The leadership of the new religious-nationalists obliterated all this. It brought to the Israeli Right a combination inherently hostile to its traditional tenets: Instead of a secular, pro-western orientation, the Gush returned to Jewish singularity, shining in its loneliness against the dark backdrop of an alleged universal rejection. Instead of the political action and international recognition, regarded by both Herzl and Jabotinsky as primary tools, the Gush created "facts" by settling the land. Yet, under the new, post-1967 circumstances, the right readily accepted this mantle and gave total support to a political ideology which was, in many respects, foreign to everything it had preached in the past.

The emphasis put by the Gush on settling the land naturally appealed to the more activist elements in the Labor movement and its various settlement organizations. Settling the land had always been more than a means toward accomplishing the Return to the Homeland. It had always been the cornerstone of the Labor Zionist ethic. Settling the land fulfilled two functions: The actual, physical act of populating the land extended the Jewish holdings in Palestine and created new sources of livelihood. The non-material aspect of settling the land provided a symbol for the Zionist revolution. It represented an act of defiance against everything that was negative—galut, parasitism, capitalism—and an affirmation of all things positive—earthiness, independence, socialism.

All Zionist youth movements, with the exception of the Revisionists, have consecrated the attachment to the soil as a hallowed commandment. Their whole educational system until very recently was aimed at bringing Jewish youth to self-fulfillment through one channel: joining a settlement. Few among Labor leadership, past and present, have not had their days in a kibbutz. In fact, the Hebrew terms depicting settlement and settlers have acquired such a unique meaning that they are hardly translatable. English equivalents are somewhat misleading since they are sometimes charged with negative connotations. The Hebrew connotations are all positive and synonymous with "pioneering," "new frontiers," "rural innocence." The very name of the Jewish community in Palestine, the Yishuv, means "settlement."

When the Gush applied this Zionist ethos to the sites of biblical Eretz Israel, when it enlisted thousands of enthusiastic idealists to carry out the traditional Zionist task of "self-fulfillment," it naturally aroused acclaim and support from many Labor circles, particularly from its powerful kibbutz and moshav movements. Some, like Moshe Shamir, former leftist author, became the secular spokesmen for the Gush, seeing in traditional Jewish elements, as distinct from Herzlian Zionism, the true force governing Jewish and Israeli history. They turned their back on the old much-shaken Labor dogma and found new solace in the renascent forces of religious-inspired nationalism.

This partnership between the secular and religious nationalists is facilitated by the fact that the religious aspect is underplayed to the point of nonexistence in Gush propaganda which is aimed at wide Israeli audiences. Emphasis is placed almost exclusively on the national, pioneering, and idealistic values of the Gush for two important reasons. Firstly, according to Gush philosophy, the nationalists and settlers within the secular camp are equal partners in the all-commanding objective of populating the land, thus helping to usher in the new Redemption. Secondly, the leaders of the Gush understand, with astute political instinct, that the state assistance they seek through grants-in-aid, government loans, military protection, and all the infrastructure needed for the settlements can only be obtained with wide support of the secular sector and its political representatives. Consequently, divisive religious issues had to be muted, thus allowing totally secular Israelis to support the Gush. This tactic notwithstanding, it should be emphasized that Gush settlers cling to their religious orthodoxy and philosophy with all the fervor expected of them.

The ideological foundation of the Gush has all the features of a panacea and their Zionism is part of a fundamentalist religious outlook. From this viewpoint, the wheel of history has gone a full turn. The Jewish people are returning to pre-Herzlian, messianic yearnings; but unlike their helplessness in the past, their present might can be used to implement their right. The demand for a Greater Israel is not dictated by security needs; it is a manifestation of a right, a duty which Jews have no authority to relinquish. The perception of Israel in the world must also undergo radical transformation. The Herzlian vision of a normalized relationship between Israel—the state and the people—and the outside world is replaced by the new interpretation given to biblical maxims. Balaam's blessing in Numbers of the people who "shall dwell alone and among the nations shall not be reckoned" is seen as a prophecy with a direct and political relevance to the Jewish state. The Return to Zion is not to be a return to the family of nations but its diametric opposite—a new polarization between the Jews and the Gentiles of the earth. Harold Fish, former rector of the religious Bar Ilan University, emphasizes this in his book *The Zionist Revolution.* According to Fish, Zionism was not a result of the emancipation of the Jews but had its foundation in

Jewish liturgy and myth. In today's post-Enlightenment world, he asks, does not the Zionism of Herzl and Weizmann "begin to look a trifle old-fashioned"?[5]

Fish, like other new religious nationalists, sees Zionism as a movement dominated by pre-Herzlian religious sentiments and spearheaded by the Orthodox immigration to Palestine. The Zionism he identifies with preceded political Zionism and had no relation to the rational, secular, and liberal trends affecting Herzlian thought.

This new perception involves more than the question of origins. In this formulation, the very status of the land Eretz Israel takes on a new mystical meaning, radically different from that attributed to it in classic Zionist thought. Even those Zionists who vehemently rejected any substitute to Zion such as Uganda—the "Palestinian Zionists" as they were called—saw the Return to Zion as the only national solution to the problems of postemancipation Jewry. The redemption was that of the people and their values, not a redemption of the land per se. Eretz Israel was the only framework within which such a solution could take place, but it was never seen as having an eschatological meaning, or as a metaphysical entity, standing above reality and beyond the needs of the people.

Israel's Declaration of Independence adopted this inherently secular view characteristic of political Zionism:

The Land of Israel was the birthplace of the Jewish people. Here their spiritual, religious, and national identity was formed. Here they achieved independence and created a culture of national and universal significance. Here they wrote and gave the Bible to the world.

But is not such a perception somewhat out-dated, according to the new post-1967 religious thinking? Is not the land itself sacred? Joel Florsheim, a religious thinker, explains how utterly mistaken was the approach of the declaration. The paragraph quoted above, he claims, is not peculiar to the Jewish people, and its contents could be applicable to all other nations: "We need only replace the terms 'Israel' and 'the Jewish people' with the parallel terms and instead of 'the Bible' insert the appropriate cultural contribution; in other words, this view expresses the Zionist yearning for normalization."[6] Florsheim shatters one by one the factual statements of the declaration. The people of Israel were not born in Eretz Israel but in Egypt and the desert, in God's words to Moses; their spiritual, religious, and national identity—from the Babylonian Talmud to Zionism itself—was formed mainly in exile, outside the land of Israel; its cultural and universal contribution was certainly the fruit of long periods of exile and dispersal when the Jews lived far from the Promised Land.

What, then, is the real status of the Land of Israel? It is based on an idea that "there is an ideological chasm between the people of Israel and the nations of the earth until this very day." Eretz Israel is a constituent part of a universal message: God Almighty is not only the Creator of the world but also King of the universe, and His Kingdom takes body in the obligation undertaken by the Jewish people in the Covenant with Abraham the Patriarch, which preordained that the Land of Canaan shall be granted as an estate in perpetuity to the seed of Abraham. This is Divine Will and Justice and without it there is no way of explaining the Jewish claim to the Holy Land and the priority of this claim over Arab right. Without this divine justification, the restitution of the land to the Jews is an irrational act spelling injustice to the Arab inhabitants of Palestine. According to this view, Zionism has committed a basic error: "It failed, because of the attempt to turn the Jewish people into something which they are not—a normal nation—and thus turn Eretz Israel into something which it is not—what every homeland is to the people living in it."

In other words, Israel's solitary position is a necessary and unavoidable outcome of the uniqueness of the Jews, a fate Zionism sought in vain to escape, and not an affliction which descended upon the state.

Another religious thinker, Chaim Peles, expresses the same

fundamentalist idea in a different vein: Zionist history is divided into three parts which are constituents of a dialectical development. The thesis is represented by the religious precursors of Zionism who preceded Herzl and spoke of the Return in exclusively observant terms; the antithesis is secular Herzlian Zionism which succeeded in creating a state but failed to infuse it with Jewish content and consequently reached, after the Yom Kippur War, a point of spiritual bankruptcy; the synthesis is the post-Yom Kippur War period which is characterized by a new religious-national renaissance. This new form of religious Zionism extends the ancient concept of commandments which are not to be contravened whatever the cost to the injunction prohibiting the relinquishing of any part of Eretz Israel. Hence it does not share, according to Peles, "the traditional anxieties of Zionism and the secular camp, who are horrified by the prospect of Israel's isolation." On the contrary, it is precisely this solitude which the Gush relishes. Balaam's blessing comes to life: Israel shall indeed dwell alone and not be reckoned by the nations and not reckon with them. This "splendid isolation" is necessary; otherwise the state might lose its right of, and sole justification for, its independent existence. Moreover, Balaam's curse-turned-into blessing is necessary in order to retain that very Jewish uniqueness "which we refused to sell for a mess of pottage."[7]

Accordingly, Israel's isolation, and even its wars, are seen as acts of divine grace. Peles says:

The reason for the prohibition to make a pact of friendship and love with the goyim is that we should not fraternize with them too much, so as not to learn from their ways. The people of Israel are presently in such a state that a formal peace with the Arabs will bring about assimilation of large parts of our people in the Semitic region. Consequently, we may see in the state of war between us and the Arabs the hand of Providence which sees to it that the integrity of the people is maintained.[8]

Rabbi Yaacov Ariel adds that the religious Jew, despite his higher moral stature, objects to peace because he retains "a

more developed historical consciousness, which does not let
him forget the events of his past and induces in him a more
cautious attitude toward the outside world." Moreover, the
opposition to peace is draped in an ideological cloak: Peace,
like the concept of Redemption, cannot be a secular, earthly
matter. Peace, like Redemption, can have only a religious messianic meaning. "Believing Jews who hold the idea of peace as a
sacred prophetic and sublime ideal are not prepared to convert
it into a phoney 'peace' of trips to the pyramids."[9]

Thus, true peace becomes a metaphysical concept involving
a millennial recognition of the absolute monotheism of the
Lord who is One, and a recognition by non-Jews of Jewish
Jerusalem as their "spiritual capital." Peace—the goal toward
which every Zionist stream and faction has always striven—is
not included in the political platform of the Gush and is relegated to a distant millennial future.

Some are not content to stop there: Aloneness is not sufficient. In order to complete the return to pre-Herzlian concepts,
the relationship between Israel and the world must be grounded
on that very "eternal hatred" between Jews and Gentiles which
Zionism sought to cure. Thus Rabbi Ephraim Zemmel describes
the conflict between Israel and the outside world as part of a
"satanic heritage" which puts every "descendent of Esau in a
consistent and perpetual ambush against the sons of Israel, so as
to hurt and destroy them when the opportunity arises." The
origins of this conflict are not to be found in mere human factors
but in the "confrontation between Good and Evil in the world of
eternity and in Satan's ambition to uproot our Holy Scriptures."
Furthermore, nothing can be done to relieve this bitter and eternal hatred. In fact, this hatred is "growing by leaps and bounds
from generation to generation." Because of this, there is no
point is seeking any political solution, as the "forces of Satan
will not abide the existence of the people of Israel" and "we
would be better off isolated from the nations of the earth."[10]
Moreover, the present conflicts of Israel are a direct continuation of biblical sagas: Israel's condemnation by the Security

Council is part of the conflict between Esau and Jacob, and the ongoing war with the Arabs is directly related to the struggle between Isaac and Ishmael.

In Gush parlance the Arabs are the Ishmaelites, Jebusites, Amalekites, and the seven Canaanite peoples against which the Pentateuch rails. Rabbi Israel Sadan claims: "The people of Israel are not like the other nations. All our efforts to integrate into the Middle East are doomed. The whole world is on the one side and we are on the other. If we forget this uniqueness, Esau and Ishmael will remind us of this fact by whips and scorpions."[11] Biblical and Halachic dicta are cited as directly applicable to Israel's security dilemmas. The Deuteronomy injunction to smite Amalek and "blot out his memory" is taken, despite all religious evidence to the contrary, as referring to the Arabs. Consequently, and because Israel's wars are described as a "war of religious obligation," ordinary rules of humanity should not be applicable to these new "Amalekites." Rabbi Menachem M. Kasher, in his post-1967 essay entitled "The Great Era," maintains that this astounding analogy should be made and that the biblical verse " . . . I will drive them out before you little by little, until you have increased and possess the land" applies to Israel's relationship with the Arabs. Military rabbinical chaplains have scandalized the public by asserting that under Halachic law, Arab civilians may be killed in these wars of religious obligation. Rabbi Israel Hess, of Bar Ilan University, went even further and unwittingly mocked his own views by resorting to Moslem terminology and declaring that "God personally intervenes in this war of religious obligation against the Amalekites and declares a counter-*Jihad* against them." Lest anyone miss the innuendo, the article, published by the Bar Ilan Students Union, is entitled "The Torah's Commandment of Genocide."[12]

In this semimystical world, where ancient quotations are taken out of their historical context and Judaism's great humanistic tradition is thrown to the wind, messianism acquires a strange interpretation, unprecedented in Jewish thought. The

millennial vision of peace to all nations and divine justice
reigning throughout the universe are left in their traditional
place—a distant era of Revealed End, a target of age-old yearnings and aspirations. On the other hand, the political reality of
Israel's existence and wars is seen as a present manifestation of
this otherwise remote vision. In the blunt language of the late
Rabbi Zvi Yehuda Kook, this messianic quality manifests itself
in every aspect of Israel's political and military might; "The
Israel Defense Army is total sanctity; it represents the rule of
the people of the Lord over his Land."[13] The territories conquered by Israel are thus also clothed in sanctity and rabbinical
pronouncements are issued with monotonous regularity pro-
claiming that the relinquishing of these lands bequeathed by
the Patriarchs is an act of sacrilege. One faction claimed that
by their interpretation of biblical sources, there is hardly room
for non-Jews in Israel. Rabbi Eliezer Waldenberg, holder of the
prestigious 1976 Israel Prize for Halachic Studies, argues that a
non-Jew should be forbidden to live in Jerusalem and that "we
should have driven all the goyim away from Jerusalem and
purified it completely."[14] Similarly, non-Jews should not be
allowed to form a majority in any Israeli city.

Thus a growing identity was established between chauvinistic and xenophobic extremism and the religious community
in Israel. However, this identification is misleading. Within
this community, as well as within the religious establishment,
there is widespread opposition to Gush philosophy and action.
Courage and Peace, a small brave group within the religious
camp, wages a constant struggle against the new militants and
accuses them of robbing Judaism of its quintessential humanistic elements. Well-known rabbis in Israel and in the Diaspora
refuse to see Israel's security problems through Halachic eyes
and controvert the theological foundation of Gush views. The
former Sephardi chief rabbi, Ovadia Yosef, disputes the edict
which prohibits the bartering of any part of Judea and Samaria
in return for peace. Within the National Religious Party, a
small but persistent minority supports the views of the dovish

Peace Now movement. Outside the National Religious Party, the ultra-Orthodox camp continues its non-Zionist tradition and emphasizes the Jewish instinct to come to terms with the world powers.

Moreover, in the wake of the war in Lebanon and the death of many yeshiva students in battle, a new mood against Gush Emunim has emerged. Demonstrations of religious people against the war—a hitherto unfamiliar sight—took place sporadically throughout the country. New voices were heard: the chief rabbi, Shlomo Goren, issued a statement denying that under Jewish Law Arabs cannot have equal rights. Reacting to extremist voices within the religious camp demanding the annexation of southern Lebanon, Rabbi Yehuda Amital, a founder of the Gush, addressed his students in the wake of the Lebanese venture and issued a call for moderation. He labeled these views which welcome war as a permanent state a blasphemy and a danger to the future of religious Judaism. Expressing his anxiety about the impact of Israel's policy on anti-Semitism and the future of Jews in the Diaspora, he declared that the interests of the people of Israel precede that of Eretz Israel. Moreover— heresy of heresies—Rabbi Amital declared that if one day there would be a chance for true peace with the Arabs, he would opt for territorial compromise and prefer "having more Jews in less land than more land with less Jews."[15] Such sentiments have greatly encouraged the more moderate elements within the religious camp.

Nevertheless, the tendency that has had the upper hand since 1967 is obvious. An appeal launched by religious academics and published in the Israeli press in 1977 calling the faithful to prayer was typical of the new mood engulfing the country.

It did not come from an obscure group of fanatics but from highly respectable religious professors at various Israeli universities, and stated:

When we ponder the root causes of Israel's difficulties, we find ourselves of necessity entertaining a sense of loneliness, in keeping with the biblical saying, "People that shall dwell alone and among the nations it shall not be reckoned," beginning with Abraham the Hebrew, "All the world on one side and Abraham on the other side" until our very days, this period of Holocaust and Revival. Our situation resembles that of the Children of Israel standing on the shore of the Red Sea, surrounded on all sides by enemies, both near and far, desirous of destroying us.[16]

The religious-nationalist message of the Gush gave an ostensibly complete answer to the question of Israel's place in history. As distinct from the soul-searching questions of Israelis who saw old foundations giving way to new doubts and ancient instincts, the Gush statement is based upon an alleged unshaken continuity of Jewish history. The power of the Gush lies therefore not only in its capacity to establish settlements but also in its capacity to place an ideological exclamation mark where questions still linger.

The power of the Synagogue Militant has been nourished by a strange alliance with the secular majority. Yet anyone reading the startling Gush quotes here and is, at the same time, familiar with Israeli society, cannot imagine a greater chasm separating the messianic zealots from the hedonistic-permissive mentality typical of large numbers of secular Israelis. In fact, the post-1967 period has created two different but characteristic responses: one presents the new fundamentalism whose symbol is Kiryat Arba. The other affirms the "good life" founded upon postwar prosperity and the growing influence of Western manners and mores. The symbol of this materialistic mood is Dizengoff Street in Tel Aviv. Basking in Mediterranean sunniness, it abounds with boutiques and sidewalk cafés. As the home of Israeli bohemian life and the place where fads and fashions are set, Dizengoff Street exudes a certain sleazy charm and enjoys an informal happy-go-lucky ambience. One cannot imagine a more dramatic visual contrast than that between Dizengoff Street and Kiryat Arba, perched as it is on the rocky hills of Hebron: Overlooking the Judean wilderness, it uneasily adjoins the devout Moslem city, defying the wind and the landscape with its stone-faced buildings and surrounded by a protective fence.

These two examples explain many features in Israeli society. In many respects, the secular Jewish majority belongs to that Western sector in which the decline of religion has reached its lowest point. No external trappings, no studies of "Jewish Consciousness" and no attachment to Judaic folklore can alter this reality. A groundswell of permissiveness pervades Israel's pop culture. Most of the products of the local movie industry, nicknamed "Dizengoff trash," border on soft porn and cross the border of good taste. Four-letter words are widely used in mass media to an extent hardly known even in most libertarian societies. Small ads in daily newspapers offer every possible diversion, from swinging couples and gay friendships to the most explicit kinky relations. Hebrew songs, popularized by radio and television, employ lyrics which should enrage religious Jews. One depicts David and Jonathan as two raving queers. Hashish and other soft drugs are tolerated in wide circles. Semipornographic publications are openly and widely circulated, and nude scenes on display posters accepted by Israelis shock many visitors.

Israelis point out that the most extreme features of permissiveness—open drug trade, hard-core pornography, gay militancy—are absent from the scene and that marriage as an undisputed institution is still prevalent. Yet it can be argued that permissive trends in Israel are more hedonistic than their western counterparts because they are devoid of any ideological content. Absent from the Dizengoff environment is any trace of the radicalism which sees in the new trend a release from arbitrary inhibitions and a move toward greater equality and true autonomy of the individual. The "Dizengoff trash" pop-culture entertains no such lofty ideals, and its typical attitude is that of a playful macho sexuality.

Permissiveness is merely one aspect of the strong secular-western influences on contemporary Israel. Fashions and fads current abroad quickly appear and acquire immediate popularity. Transcendental Meditation claims many disciples (an estimated 1 percent of the general population!) and various schools of human encounter groups, yoga, and experimental body control techniques have a high number of adherents.

The easy absorption of foreign ideas coincides with a growing secular alienation from religious injunctions. The post-1967 period has seen less Sabbath observance and more bread on Passover. Tel Aviv cinemas have broken a long tradition of shutting down on Friday nights and have begun to open their gates to eager customers on the Sabbath. Few kosher restaurants exist outside the hotels which cater to tourists. Enrollment in religious schools, despite all the clamor about the revival of the faith and the publicity given to "born again" Jews, is on the decline and went down from 33 percent in 1959/60 to 25 percent in 1982/83. Indeed, the recent decade has seen two contrasting phenomena: a hardening religious militancy and a movement to bring secular "repentants" back to the fold on the one hand, and a growing secular hedonism on the other.

Between these two, however, there has hardly been any ideological clash. The Dizengoff milieu is neutral in the crucial war being waged for Israel's soul; Kiryat Arba is obsessed with its struggles for a Greater Israel and chooses to ignore these ephemeral goings-on. Between the worlds of Kiryat Arba and Dizengoff Street a silent truce prevails.

How could this truce have been achieved? How could a secular majority guilty of breaking major Judaic commandments and a determined fundamentalist group coexist? By its readiness to move out of town and into settlements, Gush has symbolized the continuation of the old pioneering values. Here, in an age of growing individualism and materialism, is a group which continues the proud tradition. But admiration for such qualities is not explanation enough. The ultra-Orthodox elements of Mea Shearim are as idealistic in their own way as is the Gush, living as they do in abject poverty, totally dedicated to their beliefs, shunning any state assistance. One obvious explanation is that the ultra-Orthodox are non-Zionists and stand apart in their manners, dress, and behavior from the mainstream of Israeli society. Gush youngsters are the familiar Sabras who keep up the customary features of pioneer life.

But there is more to this coexistence than these superficial appearances. The Gush and its followers do not hinder the secular majority in its enjoyment of the good life. Gush demands are aimed at targets outside the interests of the average Israeli. The Gush wants governmental assistance, land for its settlements, funds for its settlers. Its chauvinistic philosophy is directed at Israel's real and alleged enemies and is not felt by the general public. Unlike the ultra-Orthodox, Gush does not interfere with the secular majority's way of life. It does not threaten transportation or soccer games on the Sabbath. It lets the majority live its own life and enjoy its pleasures and demands allegiance only on one issue—the settlement of Eretz Israel. With the establishment of dormitory suburbs in Judea and Samaria, a community of interests between the two camps was established. What the Gush advocated for ideological reasons could now be translated into pragmatic terms: inexpensive housing, a short distance from the cities of Jerusalem and Tel Aviv, enticing ordinary Israelis with promises of "quality of life" and "roads bypassing Arab villages."

This does not mean that among Gush regulars there is a readiness to live together with the nonobservant; on the contrary, almost all attempts at joint settlements, uniting Gush and secular settlers, have failed miserably and often come to open quarrels. But this fact certainly does not hurt the secular majority's pursuit of its own interests. The Gush readiness to turn a blind eye to sacrilege and transgression lies in its total preoccupation with the settlement of the Land of Israel to the exclusion of other Judaic tenets. For the sake of this objective, it is permissible to ignore sins and heresies of the gravest nature. He who supports their politics gains not only their sympathy but also the sanction and acclaim of their religious leaders and sages. All other Halachic aspects are disregarded.

Thus, at Gush yeshivas, receptions which had always been reserved for great figures of religious learning are staged for generals and politicians who have never seen the inside of a synagogue. No sin, even flagrantly committed in public, will diminish the adulation rendered by Gush rabbis to their secular partners. And, conversely, God-fearing and observant Jews are boycotted and ostracized by Gush fanatics if they hold dovish views. Thus, members of the Courage and Peace group, who advocate territorial concessions in return for peace, have been prevented from holding a meeting at a religious kibbutz or conducting services at a Jerusalem synagogue.

This is not merely a matter of political expedience. Although Gush people are scrupulously observant, they have not hesitated to openly justify their overlooking of breaches of religious laws. Rabbi Moshe Levinger, of Kiryat Arba fame, thus explained why Omri, father of Ahab, was worthy of becoming king of Israel, despite the fact that, according to the Book of Kings, he "did what is evil in the eyes of the Lord, and did worse than all that were before him." Omri "bought Mount Samaria, of Shemer, for two talents of silver, and built on the mount, and called the name of the city which he had built after the name of Shemer, the lord of the mount, Samaria." Under Labor rule, Rabbi Levinger called upon cabinet ministers to heed this precedent and desist from their opposition to the settling of Samaria.[17]

What can the secular Israeli understand from such an admonition? The answer, says the writer Ehud Ben Ezer, is that secular Jews, like King Omri, have an easy choice: They can break the law, do all that is evil in the eyes of the Lord and buy their indulgence by supporting Gush settlements. All their sins shall be cleansed providing they lend a hand to building a city in Samaria.[18]

Thus Kiryat Arba can dwell alongside Dizengoff Street. On a different level, this coexistence has a more fundamental meaning. Both signify a retreat from the traditional Zionist credo, which aspired to bring the Jews back to a normal national existence while retaining their identity. Kiryat Arba renounces this composite vision and its inner tension by putting exclusive trust in the Almighty and by annulling the obligations which derive from Israel's membership in the family of nations. Dizengoff Street relinquishes this vision by sinking into the pleasures and the preoccupations of the moment. Despite this contrast, neither makes demands of the other side and all their grievances are directed toward the world at large. Not for them is inner torment, doubt, and self-questioning.

The continued existence of this alliance between the Gush and a large number of secular Israelis obviously is based on mutual convenience. Indeed, when inflation and recession began looming large under Begin's government, in early 1981, the Gush became distinctly less popular because of its demands on dwindling public funds. It regained its public standing only after the government changed its economic policy and raised the standard of living and levels of consumption through deficit spending.

Moreover, the Gush takes a lenient view of secular misdeeds. The readiness to consecrate King Omri of the Bible with General Sharon can be seen as a flight from the real struggle for the soul of Israeli Jews. In that real arena, where faith has to combat freethinking and observance has to wrestle with permissiveness, the Gush philosophy is doomed, and its proponents must carry their struggle to the political sphere where they can easily acquire secular allies. The Land of Israel is raised to a pedestal of unquestioned sanctity; all else is forgotten and forgiven.

The writer A. B. Yehoshua commented:

Placing the concept of Greater Israel at the center of the struggle of certain religious circles is actually a desperate attempt on their part to halt the process of deep secularization taking place within the Jewish people from the beginning of this century.... Since these circles are aware that reforming Israel's society in the spirit of the Torah and the Halachah has become a "mission impossible," they try to bind Israel's society to them by way of a national challenge of a religious tinge.[19]

In the middle of Israel's political and ideological spectrum stands a large part of the public, partner neither to Kiryat Arba's messianism nor to Dizengoff Street's hedonism. But this silent mass can hardly find a political expression. Shinui, the Movement for Change, which sprang up after the Yom Kippur War and of which the author was a founder, aimed at giving this public a political voice. But its objectives were frustrated by the merger into the Democratic Movement for Change under Yigael Yadin's leadership. With its eventual decision to join Begin's cabinet, it lost its capacity for effective action. The Peace Now movement which spontaneously came into being after Sadat's visit to Jerusalem also serves as a spokesman for this sane public. However, because it is an extra-parliamentary group, its efficacy is limited.

The ascendancy of fundamentalist militancy has had a direct impact on Israel's foreign policy and international standing. The Gush is responsible not only for imposing its will on the government but also for artificially adding an aggressive religious side to Israel's just war of self-defense. In truth, Israel is a tiny island of democracy fighting for survival in a hostile Arab-Moslem ocean. But this truth is clouded by the assertions and actions of Gush. Within Israeli society this new activism, despite all the sincere idealism it demonstrates, has had an unsettling influence, as can be seen in an incident which took place near Nablus on January 5, 1980. As Agriculture Minister Ariel Sharon, the patron of the Gush, was returning by car from Elon Moreh—the controversial settlement established near Nablus—his way was blocked by a demonstration of Peace Now youths, who barricaded the road and would not let the minister's motorcade proceed in protest against the minister's aggressive policies. For many tense hours, the two parties faced each other, on a desolate road in a barren patch of Samaria. Gush settlers came down and threatened to forcibly remove the road block. Television crews rushed to the scene from Jerusalem ready to capture the confrontation. From a safe distance, on the surrounding hillsides, Arab shepherds stood watching in silence. Army units were brought in for any eventuality. Finally several senior officers arrived by helicopter and managed to negotiate a peaceful resolution. The minister's motorcade was allowed to drive on. Forgotten in the excitement was one fact: The minister's visit to the Gush settlement and the whole incident took place on the Sabbath, when under Jewish law driving is strictly banned.

8

THE END OF THE SABRA MYTH

THE mold into which the native-born Hebrew was cast had been shaped before his birth. He was destined to be everything the diaspora Jew was not: a rooted peasant, a native son, an earthy tiller of the soil. The first generation of Hebrew children born in the new land were called Sabras after the local cacti. With their birth a cult was born: the cult of the Sabra, the prickly pear which is rough on the outside but which has, if you manage to cut through the thorns, a sweet heart inside. The Sabras grew up with this image in their minds, implanted by their Diaspora parents. Upon his immigration to Palestine, Uri Zvi Greenberg, one of Israel's leading poets, described in a poem written in 1928, a seaside scene where "Jewish mothers have brought their children to the sun, to tan and redden the blood that paled in all the ghettoes of the Gentile world."[1] Indeed, the Sabras were often described as the children of the newly-cherished sun. In a poem devoted to the Sabra, the poet Yaacov Cohen wrote:

> We are what we are, Sabras
> Simple folk
> Sons of the sun and honest are we
> Ours is a wild charm
> And he who understands us
> will love us.[2]

Love indeed surrounded the Hebrew-speaking native-born. Their every word was recorded with amazement, their virtues extolled with a fondness rooted in the great Jewish yearning to put an end to exile. The Sabra will not only be a new man, a super Jew, but will also put an end to his parents' helplessness. One of the first Sabra protagonists in the new Hebrew literature is Amram in Joseph Chaim Brenner's novel *From Here and There*, written in 1911. The boy's unarmed father was murdered by an Arab thief. A certain verse from the Bible remains imprinted in Amram's mind: "If the thief is found breaking in, and is struck so that he dies, there shall be no bloodguilt for him." He hears about the custom of blood vengeance among the Arabs. The Jewish state of total helplessness finds expression in Amram's thoughts:

Had it been he, Amram, who had found the thief he would have torn him to pieces like a fish. And when he grows up he would become the chief watchman in the settlement. He would kill all the thieves . . . for the thief there is no bloodguilt . . . his blood required no vengeance . . . but . . . but—Father? Father was not a thief. Father was a saint. Everybody said that. . . . His father had been killed on the road. On the road. From the neighboring village. Father had not been "breaking in." On the road. And why, then, not redeem his blood? Why was the blood of his sainted father not being redeemed? Was there no one to do it?[3]

In the last chapter, the boy and his grandfather, having buried Amram's father, stand "on guard for life," and the book ends on a note of anticipation that Amram, the native-born, will avenge his father's blood: "The account is not yet settled." The grandfather who has lost his son pins his hopes on the grandson of his dreams.

Paradoxically, the image of the native son was linked from the outset to the very past he was supposed to shake off. The Jewish parent was the negative image, but his humiliation and degradation had to be avenged; the new Sabra is born with an un-Jewish image, but his very raison d'être is to build a home for menaced Jews.

This ambivalence toward their parents' past is not uncharacteristic of any first generation immigrant. What was unique about the Sabra mentality was the absence of any society, any culture, into which the Sabras could assimilate and whose ways they could emulate. Once the gate east toward the local Arab society was found shut and locked, they had to form their own personality and create their own society. According to the Sabra mystique, the native-born had therefore to grow up without any reference to a Jewish past, without ancestors, without any literary pedigree. The Sabra was born into a vacuum with no father image, only an abstract, communal "I" posited as a paragon and linked to a Jewish heritage mainly by the urge to reject it. Thus in one of the most famous biographies depicting the pre-state Yishuv, Moshe Shamir's loving memorial to his dead brother Elik, the opening phrase is: "Elik was born from the sea." Indeed in most Sabra literature written in the thirties and forties, the absence of parents and family is perhaps its most conspicuous feature. Sabras are on their own and their allegiances are divided between their commitment to Zionism and their love for each other.

The epic heroes of S. Yizhar, a leading Sabra author, strike roots in the arid ground, with none of their sustenance being derived from the wellsprings of previous generations. In the words of one critic, they are in a state of "eternal adolescence." They are men who refuse to part with their unripe youth and their childish egocentrism. Indeed, for the archetypical Sabra the adolescent state is a comfortable one: It suits his inability to adopt the image of his father, as well as his difficulties in creating an independent maturity for himself.

This childishness and egocentrism—apparent even when the Sabra is prepared to lay down his life for others—are found in practically all the Sabra literary heroes up to recent years. The Sabra is an eternal child because there is no father in whose footsteps he can follow and because the Sabra prototype is a childish figure created and fostered by this very nonexistent father. Sabras refuse to grow up mainly because they are happy the way they are.

In Moshe Shamir's classical Sabra novel, *He Walked*

Through the Fields, Uri is the expected prototype: a boy who never grew up, who is full of endearing perplexity, whose relationship to the people around him is somewhat vague and hazy. He dies carrying out the supreme mission, sacrificing himself for his comrades; yet through the entire book he hardly changes and his reactions to the people and events surrounding him remain passive and quiescent. Countless novels, plays, and poems depict the new Hebrew, the boyish man, the parentless comrade, the inarticulate hero whose encounters with the world in which he lives have the ring of primal experience. If his parents suffer from the pain of severed roots, his new earthy rootedness is coupled with a constant search for "meaning" with which he is intellectually unequipped to grapple.

It may be argued that this literary prototype never truly did justice to the young generation of the native-born. Unlike the literary image, the Sabras did have parents—many of them Yiddish-speaking immigrants who brought with them the customs and mementoes of the old world. While the fictional Sabra usually lives on the land, working the soil, most Sabras—even in pre-state times—were born and bred in urban communities and acquired urban professions. Unlike their cult counterparts, the young men and women of the Yishuv had to grow up, attain maturity, face reality and, in the end, become parents themselves.

Yet, as is the rule in such cases, the image, based on a mixture of facts and ideology, produces its own reality. Life, if it does not always follow art, becomes interwoven with it. The Sabra image, like the all-American male, did become a model figure, a yardstick by which the young Sabras measured themselves.

This pervasive phenomenon, the boyish manliness and alienation from the world of the old-timers, explains two distinctive features of the Sabra generation: their failure to take over leadership positions and their incestuous attachment to "the gang," the nuclear group of friends which dominates Israel's social scene. The failure of the Sabras to assume leadership positions is too conspicuous to be glossed over. More than thirty years after

independence, and a hundred years after the beginning of the
Jewish settlement of Palestine, Israel has had only one Sabra
prime minister—Yitzchak Rabin—who came into office when
Labor was looking for someone not involved in the Yom Kippur
fiasco, and who stepped down after three years, bringing the
Labor party down with him. For successive generations of the
native-born, the division of labor with the parental old-timers
was taken for granted. The parents, symbolized by such dominant figures as Ben Gurion, Golda Meir, Menachem Begin, all
born in the Diaspora, are the decision makers; the Sabra sons
serve, at best, as their adjutants and usually carry out the decisions made for them. They have no ideology of their own, nor
are they capable of organizing so they could lock horns with
their elders. The tacit understanding in both the Yishuv and
Israel is that the Sabra generation will be allowed into positions
of leadership only after the old-timers have departed from the
scene.

   Sociologist Yonathan Shapiro, an astute observer of the political scene, explains the origins of this apparition of the
manly Sabra who is a political neuter:

This placed the native-born in an extremely difficult situation. Unlike the young Jews who had grown up abroad in confrontation with
the older generation, incapable of finding a solution to the Jews' wors-
ening situation, the native-born found themselves confronting an
older generation imbued with success at having accomplished its
goals. . . . In consequence, the young people did not challenge the
Zionist and Socialist theses of the generations of the founders. The
native-born youth were thus unable to crystalize into generation units
with nuclei groups capable of adopting independent world views.
However, when they grew up, they found that the organizational and
political structures set up by the elders were closed to them. For lack
of any other alternative, they were compelled to organize themselves
but they were an abortive generation without an independent world
view . . . conspicuous in its weakness and sterility.[4]

   From the early formative days of the Yishuv, the young Sabra
has regarded himself not only as a new creature cut off from his

ancestral roots but also instinctively excluded from the ruling elite. It is his duty to perform what the country, the nation, the community expect: to be a farmer or a soldier, to build, to sow, to do battle and to die, if necessary. He must fulfill a mission—*shelichut* is the Hebrew term—wherever and whenever the call comes. He is the *shaliach*, the one who goes out on a mission, not the one who decides what the mission is. The anthem of the Palmach, the Yishuv's underground units and the breeding-ground of Sabra folklore, is characteristic of this mood: It starts with a proclamation that "we are the first ones" to go anywhere and ends with the statement "let the Old Man only say the word." The Old Man, in this case, was the legendary Polish-born Yitzchak Sadeh, commander of the Palmach, but the phrase itself could be applicable to a whole generation of old men whose word the "first ones" await.

With alienation from the parental home, the immigrants' first-generation syndrome compounded by the special Sabra credo, and with exclusion from political leadership, the classical Sabra sinks, in fact as well as in fiction, into the *chevrah*, his own group of close friends. The hallmark of the chevrah is total mutual loyalty and involvement in each other's life. This honeycomb nature of Sabra society is an obtrusive fact of life and is routinely celebrated, and ridiculed, in Israeli literature. Thus, Amos Kennan, a noted satirist, wrote a grotesque obituary to Dani, a Sabra who took his own life:

Once there was a tragedy. The entire gang went out of town to attend the wedding of one of its members, and Dani was left by himself. All evening he walked the streets alone and didn't meet anybody. This made him despondent. He killed himself for this reason, and to this day no one knows how he managed to do it all by himself.[5]

A similar mood of in-group obsessiveness pervades Moshe Shamir's homage to his brother Elik, the Sabra "born from the sea."[6] This book achieves a truly classic description of a new type of hero: the kind-hearted, grass-roots Sabra, the child of the sun and soil of Eretz Israel. Yet, what most typifies Elik as a person is the fact that he is an integral part of a close-knit whole. He lives and breathes with them—at the agricultural high school he attends, in the underground, or on a visit to the big city. Together with his friends, Elik discovers that they are not interested in anything except each other, that the place of the individual was increasingly being taken by companionship, and that without the group and its camaraderie life has no meaning. It has been noted that "for all his charm, talent, and resourcefulness, Shamir's Elik is devoid of any critical sense and any self-image. He adapts to the environment through a peculiar kind of conformism, not as an influencer but as someone who is influenced."[7]

A young Sabra poet, Assaf Or, gives a poignant expression to the intensity of this life in groups:

We don't like to be alone; we literally breathe each other. What does "I" mean? If you have some good jokes to tell, everybody has already heard them all. If you try and keep some secrets to yourself, everybody already knows them. If you try and hide from the group, if you try to be "different" it won't do you one bit of good, because everyone already knows you, pal.

And there is no running away from this captive friendship:

If one day you get sick of it all
And want to dream a dream that's yours and yours alone
All of a sudden you find that you're dreaming in the first
    person plural—first and plural.

Because of this, successive Sabra generations have found service in the underground and later in the army an outlet for both their dedication to the country and their unconsummated energy. In the army, the Sabra mentality could easily adjust to the ground rules: life in small units, the inherent camaraderie, the political decisions being made by somebody else.

But, over all these attributes looms one phenomenon: the

relation of Sabra to his "inferior step-brother" from the Diaspora.

Throughout the formative years of Sabra culture, in the thirties and forties and up to and including the first years of statehood, the image of the new Hebrew was always juxtaposed against his shadowy kinsman, the Diaspora Jew. It was this contrast which gave sustenance to the Sabra's self-image. The depth of this attitude can be fathomed by the fact that it survived the Holocaust and extended to the refugees from the death camps who clamored to get into the closed Sabra society. In their book, *The First Million Sabras*, Margalit Banai and Herbert Russcol described "this still unsettled breed, this still inchoate genus," and made the following observation:

> The Sabra's complex feelings toward Jews abroad are colored by the fact that he can never grasp, although he knows the sad answers, why six million Jews let themselves be murdered by the Nazis. He never can understand why they did not die on their feet. This haunts him. It is a slur on his honor. It accounts for the one profound, centrifugal trait of the Sabra: his readiness to act to defend his freedom. It has radically altered the Jewish conception of power and force; force was the Czar, who owned the Cossacks, who beat the Jews, therefore force was evil. For the Sabra, the power of force has lost its evil nature, and the importance of this shift in Jewish mentality is difficult to exaggerate.[8]

This statement was not unique. At least in the initial period of statehood, such preposterous statements, actually accusing the Jews of going to the gas chambers like sheep to the slaughterhouse, abounded in Sabra literature.

While the Jews were being led to their death, they were being accused by some Yishuv leaders of shameful passivity. Thus, Yitzchak Greenbaum, in charge of the Yishuv's rescue operations, commented that the news about the Jewish uprising in the Warsaw Ghetto lifted a weight from his heart: "We could not understand up to now how the Jews of Poland were going to death like sheep to the slaughter. Did the [Nazi] hangmen succeed in murdering their souls before they led their bodies to be slain?"[9]

Such utterances represented an extreme position, but the general sentiment of the Yishuv was that rebellion was a means of saving Jewish honor, and the victims' passivity puzzled and disturbed the native-born.

The Sabras' attitude toward the refugees of the Holocaust was tinged by these sentiments. Ehud Ben Ezer commented that "the Sabra detested the Jewish 'refugees,' who arrived after the Holocaust, who did not even speak Hebrew, whose shorts reached their knees and whose manners were a sign of weakness and effeminate frailty."[10]

Many novels describe this clash. In Shamai Golan's *The Death of Uri Peled*, the protagonist came to the country as a young escapee from the Holocaust. Like many new immigrants, he acquires a Sabra name as well as Sabra mannerisms. Nevertheless, he is viewed with suspicious disdain by the homogeneous native society he encounters. His friend, a fifth generation Sabra, harangues him:

The fighters of our War of Independence died for you, so that this land could absorb the likes of you—refugees who arrive from many exiles. We spilled our blood for this country, and you, I'm telling you, don't you now turn it into a pigsty with your swinish galut wheeling and dealing.[11]

In these typically harsh words is the very duality, the ambivalence, which characterized in those early years the mentality of the Sabra: He is ready to die for those he despises. The same attitude pervades many children's books on which the young are reared today. The Jewish immigrant boy, seeking the company of the healthy Sabras, is always portrayed as a pale weakling, gradually losing his ashen look and acquiring true manly Sabra qualities. Occasionally, there is some feeling of remorse among the local boys when their nastiness toward the newly arrived orphans is overdone. One such story tells of the typical Jewish boy: "pallid, wearing strange clothes . . . his seemingly bloodless face round like a girl's . . . his hair well combed above his white and smooth forehead." In short, the very opposite of the sun-tanned macho gang which accords him a typical welcome of ridicule: "My word, he is funny." The galut boy, who "squirms and shakes all over" when he hears the sound of a plane in the sky, becomes friendly only with one of the boys, "who is also somewhat strange."[12] In his eagerness to be accepted by the Sabra gang, the refugee boy claims that he can swim like everybody else. In order to prove this, he dives into the pool and nearly drowns; he is saved in the nick of time by his stunned companions. Such remorse is rare in Israeli children's literature.

The ordinary scheme is depicted in a book entitled *The Funny One with the Earrings*. Any Israeli child who sees this title instinctively knows that "the funny one with the earrings" can only be the strange, funny-looking new immigrant Jewish girl. The book tells about the trials and tribulations of the usual pale girl who watches the frolicking Sabras "with the big dark eyes of a wounded animal." The Sabras welcome her, as is their wont, by hanging a sign reading "I'm an ass" on her and by similar mischievous pranks. But the girl acculturates with amazing speed. She removes the earrings, acquires the customary sloppiness and begins to resort to the slurring drawl of the Sabra. At the end of the book she has achieved the supreme Sabra status symbol of defiantly talking back to her father.

These random illustrations underscore the Sabra feeling of superiority over his allegedly negative Jewish twin. The "negation of Exile" is expressed, in Sabra folklore, by a paternalistic attitude, oscillating between pity and contempt, toward the typical representative of that Exile. In the fifties, when the refugees from Nazi Europe were sharing the crowded transition camps with the refugees from Islamic repression, the Sabra cult reached its zenith and the Canaanites, who rejected the very nexus between Jews and Israelis, were reaching the peak of their influence. For a time it seemed that Sabra chauvinism was impervious to what had happened to European Jews.

Some of the refugees, in typical Jewish fashion, assimilated into this brash environment with great vigor, and a few even managed to out-Sabra the local specimen. Suppressing their nightmarish memories, parentless and homeless in a society dominated by familial ties, these refugee children acquired new Sabra names and personalities. Some became Sabra gurus, offering famous morsels of native humor and folklore. Dahn Ben Amotz, the classic refugee-turned-Sabra, described this process. After changing his galut name for the "obligatory Sabra Hebrew name" he was born anew:

With one blow I severed my links with my private past, to such an extent that I began to be born in Palestine—to invent a new identity, to deny any connection with my factual biography. With time the new identity I acquired became my authentic identity. . . . Within a few years, my Hebrew became more Sabra-sounding than that used by the native-born. Camouflaging my true past had to be perfect if I wanted people to believe my invented past.[13]

Thus, like assimilated Jews before him, Dahn Ben Amotz became more Israeli than the Israelis: "It was I, like other refugee children, who first shook off a literary Hebrew replete with galut European images, and when I began writing I resorted to the spoken substandard Hebrew which became an integral part of my identity."

The Holocaust and father's home were being blotted out of memory and replaced by all the paraphernalia of the new culture: youth movement, folklore, kibbutz life, uninhibited camaraderie, toughness mitigated by the famous below-surface sentimentality.

But this heyday of Sabra consciousness was not destined to last. Even before the Six-Day War, cracks began to appear in the seemingly solid wall. The Jewish fate, ostensibly excluded forever from the sunny shores of Israel, crept back (perhaps it merely seemed to have crept back) through the back door of Israel's external conflicts. Dormant memories of the Holocaust surfaced from the limbo of depressed nightmares into an awakened realization that the unthinkable did take place and that some explanation had to be found for it.

The new-born Sabras, the ex-refugee orphans, were beginning to relive what they could no longer suppress: childhood in
the shtetl; the last mementoes of a family which disappeared
into the abyss; survival in the face of annihilation and death.
The nightmarish screams, up to then muffled for shame of the
chevrah began to acquire literary manifestations. In 1963, a
play called *Children of the Shadow*, written by Ben Zion To-
mer, an orphan-turned-Sabra, depicts for the first time the
clash between Israeli society and the newcomers. The play's
protagonist, like the author, is an acculturated Sabra flaunting
a classic Sabra name, Yoram. But behind this healthy, earthy
mask, in constant terror, lies Yossele, the real Yiddish name of
the "child of the shadow." Yossele-Yoram is ready to look
inward beyond the Sabra mask, face his past, and recall half-
forgotten memories. The play ends with Yossele-Yoram, having survived the crisis of this new recognition, acquiring a new
balanced self-awareness of himself as a composite personality
combining traditionally Jewish with Sabra traits. The Sabra
hero, the super Jew, is no longer the opposite of the inferior
Jew. *Children of the Shadow* opened the gate to a flood of such
suppressed memories. Out of the newly acquired Hebrew
names emerged the old galut names; Yiddish phrases cropped
up; mother's last look registered; childhood scenes in the old
country recreated. The past could no longer be pushed aside.

In Aharon Appelfeld's short stories and novels the pre-Holocaust galut home is seen not only with pangs of nostalgia but
with love for a lost happy childhood; the new Israeli environment cannot compensate for the intense feelings aroused by
these resurging memories of the loved home which went up in
flames.

These new moods coincided with other cracks in Sabra tradition. Literature and folklore, both in Israel and abroad, portrayed a generation which was slowly disappearing from the
Israeli scene. The typical Sabra has always been depicted as an
Ashkenazi son of European parents. Mass immigration brought
to the Israel of the fifties hundreds of thousands of refugees

from Arab countries with non-Sabra traits: religious belief, traditional ways of life, patriarchal patterns, an emotional rejection of the Arab. While, in the fifties, Hebrew literature was hankering after the all-Israeli Sabra hero—plain, pure and patriotic—Israeli society itself was gradually changing its demographic face. To the new arrivals from North Africa and other Moslem countries, the Sabra image was so remote that even attempts at assimilation were inconceivable. Thus Shimon Blass, an author who came to Israel after statehood from Iraq where he had already been writing in Arabic, said: "The Sabra concept, being an Ashkenazi term, is irrelevant to the Oriental Israeli. 'Sabra' is synonymous with the 'beautiful Israeli' while the Oriental Jews are identified with the ugly Jew who is part of the East and consequently merits contempt."[14]

With the changing structure of Israeli society, Sabra culture became increasingly irrelevant, dealing as it did more with past glories than with present woes. In Sabra tradition, in addition to Ashkenazi heroes, the kibbutz was the center of creation. In real life, urban slums teeming with new immigrants from the Arab Diaspora loomed large among the country's social problems.

In traditional Sabra folklore, the hero is a fearless fighter who, far from hating his Arab enemy, pities him as a fellow victim, a partner in a suffering inflicted by an unnecessary war. The literature of the War of Independence abounds with such sentiments. Actually, as Amos Elon has demonstrated in *The Israelis: Founders and Sons*, these sentiments, in which the Arab refugee is the real sufferer earning the author's empathy, dominated the post-1948 literature. But, gradually, this Sabra cult began to disintegrate under the pressures of a continuous and interminable war. While the Sabra continued to project his famed invincibility overseas and in many popular novels and detective stories the young Israeli appeared as a facsimile of Ari Ben Canaan of *Exodus* fame—preventing international catastrophes, serving their country as superspies, ruthlessly stamping out terrorism through Entebbe-like operations—within Israel a different story was taking place. With war and siege becoming a permanent feature of Israeli life, the heroic sentiments of 1948 were beginning to fade. Far from ruthless fearlessness, new Sabra writings manifested a sense of deep futility and resigned despair, perhaps singular in its intensity. In vain will one look for anything resembling flag-waving patriotism. Many Sabras write "war poems," and in a great many of these, they foresee their own death. But unlike Rupert Brooke who, in World War I wrote that "if I should die, think only this of me: That there's some corner of a foreign field that is forever England," the Israeli poets find no such consolation. Death in war is seen as wholly arbitrary. Thus wrote kibbutz member Yosef Sarig a short time before he died in the Yom Kippur War:

> My death came to me suddenly
> And I cannot remember whether it happened
> In the thunder of fire or between
> The screaming walls of steel.
> Or perhaps in white, in the finally
> Silent white.
> Now
> I do not remember.[15]

And Gideon Rosenthal, who died in the same war, wrote:

> I did not support dead friends
> And I did not hear mothers weeping
> And I did not smell the stench of dead bodies
> And I did not see dismembered limbs
> But I did live twenty years
> Upon this good earth . . .

> There are those who die when they are young.
> How stupid.
> Not in bed but from a rifle's fire.
> How stupid.
> For the sake of parents whose life will be so bitter.
> How stupid.
> They die when they are only twenty.
> Only twenty.[16]

And another poet, who died in the War of Attrition along the Suez Canal, Be'eri Hazak, predicted his own death in a tank in the form of a radio dialogue between God and himself:

> Please shut your eyes now.
> I hear you now. Roger.
> You can finally die.
> Bereaved Father, I can feel no longer.
> The tears of winter will say kaddish over your grave.[17]

The sentiments expressed by these astounding poems, not written for publication, extend beyond mere private anxieties. Even when expressing political dissent, Sabra authors write about their own predicted death. Poet Meir Wieseltier writes about his own hypothetical death in a terrorist act and demands that this death not be exploited to undermine his political belief:

> If I die one day from a bullet
> Of a young Palestinian killer, who will
> Cross the Northern border or from the blast
> Of a hand grenade
> Or from the explosion of a charge
> While staring at the price of cucumbers
> In the market, do not dare say
> That my blood furnishes proof
> Of the justice of your errors
> That my torn eyes strengthen you in your blindness.[18]

During the war in Lebanon, which for the first time divided the nation and the army, these sentiments were exacerbated by a growing sense of fury and despair. During the war *Ha'aretz* published a letter to the editor from a soldier at the front, addressed at General Sharon: "You may have misunderstood me, Sharon. You move flags and shift soldiers. . . . You must be enjoying this game . . . but it kills me."[19] By the time the letter was printed, its author had been killed in action.

This constant foreboding stems not only from the fear of imminent death; the tragedy emanates from deeper sources.

The secular native-born finds himself torn by the existential dilemma characteristic of contemporary Israel. He is the product of prevailing western culture, and with his Occidental counterparts he shares modern interests and attitudes. His head reaches to the heights of secular modernity: the attraction of the sciences and the arts, the pleasures and discontents of twentieth-century civilization. Yet his legs straddle a land subject to an ancient dispute. His heart is torn between the obvious need to defend his home, private as well as national, and the dark suspicion that this battle is acquiring, in spite of himself, the character of a religious war. Had he been fanatically religious, were he ready to give his life for the Tomb of the Patriarchs in Hebron, it all would have been much simpler. But his universal-secular upbringing makes it far from simple. Hence, the sense of futility, of frustrated lives terminated by an irrelevant death. This does not mean that he casts doubts about the justice of his own cause or that he will not go to war, fight bravely, and be ready to make the supreme sacrifice, as he has always done in the past. But if the songs he prefers tend to be rather melancholy, it is perhaps because of this vague feeling that he finds himself stranded in a nightmarish existence. The Arab is not a fellow-victim, as the 1948 literature believed, but a permanent, and perhaps incorrigible, enemy. Across the barbed wire over the border lie not only tanks and minefields but also the "Lands of the Jackal"—to use Amos Oz's phrase—where unmitigated hate threatens to engulf the tiny island of Israel with its dark waves. For a brief moment peace with Egypt seemed to have built a bridge across the abyss, but its life expectancy is now subject to gnawing doubts and its failure to change general Arab attitudes is always present in the mind.

Above all, the real tragedy lies in the fact that his personal sacrifice is part of a strange and unique historical process: he, the liberated Sabra, who was supposed to represent the new Hebrew, the Israeli who would take his fate into his own hands, finds himself suddenly pondering his own Jewish destiny. He has no exhaustive explanation for this singular fate and for his unique aloneness. And, worse than that, he begins to suspect that all he learned about the Jewish past, about galut and its Jews, is losing its validity. It is this aspect which rattles the very truisms on which the Sabra mentality is grounded.

The ashen world of Auschwitz began to re-emerge in Sabra literature in the sixties. And so the galut began to creep onto the literary scene: first through childhood memories of the immigrant-turned-Sabra, then through a re-examination of the very attitude to the "inferior step-brother." A new trend, coined "neo-Jewish," began to manifest itself in the writings of native-born, authentic Sabra authors. In this new school, the galut existence is rarely shown in a negative light. On the contrary, in many of these new writings, the galut Jew appears as a forceful character, and traditional Judaism is portrayed as a powerful and consistent antidote to the Sabra's perennial perplexity. Occasionally, the roles are reversed: the galut Jew represents the stable element, the ability to weather the vicissitudes and vagaries of time and place, while the Sabra is depicted as the weak man whose disappointment with Israeli society is coupled with an immature helplessness which long ago lost its endearing qualities.

In *Nor the Battle to the Strong,* a novel by Ehud Ben Ezer, an Israeli student goes into a depression while serving his annual reserve duty in the army. He runs amok straight into the invisible enemy's fire. But before his death, he mourns his fate and bewails the tragedy of his country: "You said: a new truth. But we were cheated and became slaves to the sword, not its masters." And the heresy continues: "I wish I were unrooted, like a Jew, and not belong so much, because the roots entangle my legs and ensnare me."[20]

Similarly, in *The Bottle Parables,* by Benjamin Tammuz, one of the guiding lights of the Canaanite movement in the fifties, the galut Jew appears as hero. He is an old man who spends his twilight years in London writing booklets in Yiddish, singing the glories of the Jewish people dispersed among the Gentiles. Judaism to this old Jew is the true power and its strength lies in its very weakness, its being a non temporal force: "Everything which is spiritual, everything which is cultural is actually Jewish."[21]

In Amos Oz's novel, *A Perfect Peace*, this mood reaches a dramatic climax. Yoni, a member of a kibbutz and a son and heir to one of its founding fathers, typifies the perplexed Sabra. After much soul searching, he finally leaves the kibbutz and his wife. His place is taken by a newcomer. Azariah is the immigrant-refugee from the Diaspora. His resourcefulness and determination are juxtaposed against Yoni's ditherings and vacillations. At the end, Azariah replaces Yoni—as heir to a proud tradition, as adopted son, as a husband, and as a father to the child Yoni failed to beget. The Diaspora Jew, and not his "superior brother" has now become the redeemer. The son of the galut—who shares with the founding fathers a richness of experience, a broadness of mind, and a passion for ideology— replaces his Sabra counter-image and it is upon him that the future of Jewish existence depends.

Such sentiments, echoing the very idea against which Zionism waged unrelenting war, could have been written only after the crucial disillusionment with the Sabra myth. When Beth Hatefutzot, the Museum of the Diaspora, opened in Tel Aviv in 1979, it began to attract young Israelis eager to absorb the wealth of material attesting to the vast richness of Jewish communities in the galut. In the post-1967 period, rootedness acquired a new meaning which the founders' generation could not contemplate. Rebels though they were, their Jewish roots were established before the rebellion. Their pain was that of severed roots, but the memories and the knowledge of things Jewish—Yiddish, a chapter of Talmud studies, the constantly repeated prayers which drove them from the synagogue—were still there. The great majority of secular Israelis have no such memories. Jewishness is remote and vague. It invades an otherwise totally profane routine on rare dramatic occasions: birth, marriage, death. Their ignorance often becomes embarrassingly apparent when they travel abroad and realize how isolated they are from the routine of a Jewish community and how unknown the religious service is to them. Their pain, if it exists at all, is not of something severed but of something absent. With the great brave hopes of utopian Zionism buried under the debris of ongoing war, their Jewishness is sensed rather than understood. They become aware of their rejected past through external pressures, and they begin to wonder whether the rejection was not too hasty.

In the forties, Hazaz wrote that when a man cannot be a Jew any more, he becomes a Zionist. By the eighties, a full circle has been completed. Many young Israelis feel that their traditional secular Zionism, with its emphasis on normalcy, has reached a dead end and that Hazaz's dictum is refuted and reversed by experience: when a man cannot be a Zionist any more (Zionist in the true Herzlian sense) he reverts to being a Jew.

Nothing demonstrates this point more dramatically than what might be called the game of the name. Changing the galut-Yiddish name into a Hebrew name has become, since the Second Aliyah, a cherished practice of the new Hebrews. It was more than a mere act of immigrant acculturation: By acquiring a Hebrew name, the galut Jew transformed himself into a new being, shorn of the humiliating load of the past. By reverting to biblical names, the names of the Hebrew kings, prophets, and soldiers, the new Hebrews were embodying that wish to forget their Diaspora existence, the very essence of Zionist philosophy. Even in picking the new names, especially first names, the new Hebrews have been careful to avoid names which had galut connotations: in the Yishuv such typically Jewish names as Abraham, Isaac, Jacob, Moshe, Aaron, Sara, Rivka, and Rachel became rare; in their place were names Diaspora Jews never used or rarely resorted to: Amos, Yoram, Nimrod, Uri, Yuval, Amnon. The two-syllable name, with the accent on the second syllable, became the staple hallmark of young Israelis and their very sound pronounced a rebellion against the foreign-sounding, Yiddish-tinged names of the parents' generation.

The trend, which began with the pioneers of the Second Aliyah, acquired pace in the twenties when David Ben Gurion became secretary general of the Histadrut. In 1922, the first general census of Histadrut members was taken and Ben Gurion used this opportunity to cajole many members into adopting appropriate Hebrew names. After he became prime minister in 1948, Ben Gurion used his authority and influence to effect massive conversion of names in the young country's political and military establishment. For Ben Gurion himself (né Gruen) the new Hebrew name signified more than mere renunciation of galut: It was an act of rebirth, for, as Ben Gurion himself used to say, he had been born anew in Palestine and his galut childhood did not count as part of his life.

Under Ben Gurion's leadership, a new unwritten rule was formulated: Senior officers in the army and in the government bureaucracy had to adopt Hebrew names. Thus, men and women of advanced age acquired a new Hebrew mantle upon entering office. Golda Meyerson lived for fifty-eight years under the name she had been born with. Upon becoming foreign minister in Ben Gurion's cabinet, she turned into Golda Meir. In similar fashion, Pinhas Kozlowsky became Minister of Finance Sapir; Yigal Sukenik became Chief of Staff Yadin; Zalman Rubashov became President Shazar; Shimon Persky became Labor leader Peres. In the fifties, under the directives of Moshe Sharett, who at the age of fifty-five forsook his well-known family name of Shertok, no diplomatic passport could be issued to a bearer of a non-Hebrew name, and the Foreign Service in its entirety—Teddy Kollek the single inexplicable exception—had to acquire new Hebrew names, relinquishing, occasionally, proud age-old Jewish family names. Officials pleading special attachment to their family names were not spared. In the army, the rule was less severe: High-ranking officers such as Chaim Laskov and Ezer Weizman were allowed to keep their non-Hebrew names, the first pleading orphancy, the second an attachment to his great uncle, Chaim Weizmann.

Occasionally, when dealing with a reluctant official, a compromise was made and a Hebrew-sounding name was agreed upon. Thus, when Yizhar Smilansky, the real name behind the famous author S. Yizhar, was sent on a diplomatic mission abroad, he refused to relinquish his family name, which he shared with his father Moshe Smilansky, pioneer author who glorified the Arab way of life under the pen name of Hawaja Mussa. After protracted argument he finally consented to have the passport issued under the name of Smilan, assuming that by omitting the foreign sounding "sky," some approximation of a Hebrew name was being achieved.

But this great wave of name-changing receded with the new soul-searching mood of the sixties. No longer was the verbal transition regarded as a symbolic act of rebirth of Israel. The old names signified the very civilization destroyed by the Nazis, and relinquishing the verbal mementoes of this civilization lost some of its former attraction.

In contemporary literature, expressions of this new mood often appear. In Yitzchak Orpaz's novel *A Home for One Man*, the protagonist, Izzi Ornan (a more Sabra-Hebrew name is hard to find) is portrayed at the beginning of the book as a true Tel Avivian submerged in the typical day-to-day problems of secular Israeli society. His uncle, whose spiritual and actual language is Yiddish, symbolizes the link with traditional Judaism. Before his death, this uncle castigates his Sabra nephew: "Remember where you came from; Sternharz is a name which one should not be ashamed of."

Sternharz is the galut name of the Sabra protagonist before being hebraized. The uncle's last will and testament is not forgotten. The nephew proceeds to recall and relive his forgotten past. Jewish tradition is symbolized by a pair of Sabbath candlesticks which the nephew inherits from the dead uncle and in which he sees the road back to his forefathers' belief. And shortly after the publication of this novel the author added his original Jewish name—Auerbuch—to his acquired Hebrew one. The poet Avoth Yeshurun—again, as Hebrew a name as can be imagined—writes: "I've changed my name, I've changed my tongue, I've changed my town." His father then appears to him in a dream and fails to recognize him. The son cries out: "I, Yechiel Alter of old/ Avoth he did not recognize." And the poet wonders:

> How did I come
> To think of changing my name,
> Which cannot be changed?
>
> Why do I long
> After the name my mother gave me
> And called me?
> My name was the only thing
> She left me, she left me.[22]

And Dahn Ben Amotz, the galut orphan whose very name is synonymous with Sabra folklore, has his second thoughts too. His old name described his family hereditary occupation: Tehilimzoogger—psalmsayer. He feels no guilt at having forsaken a name which relates to one of his forefathers kibbitzing around synagogues earning paltry kopeks for repeating the appropriate psalm. His new name signifies his freedom to bury the past. Yet the past cannot be buried:

When I turned my face back for the last time, I saw my father from afar going up in flames. But this is not the end of the story. I can deny him and refuse to utter his family name in television interviews, but I cannot forget and erase him from my memory cells. I buried my father many years ago, but only with my death will he finally die together with my mother, brothers and sisters and the sounds and smells of my distant childhood.[23]

In the post-Yom Kippur War period, the process of hebraizing names slowed down. The symbolic rebirth sounded awkward while, in the wake of the initial Israeli debacle, there was much talk of Israel reverting to the traditional role of a menaced Jewish community.

Finally, in the late seventies, the last taboo fell by the wayside: the director general of the foreign ministry was Joseph Ciechanover, who spurned the idea of hebraizing his traditional name. Amos Elon, who hebraized his name in an earlier age and in a different national mood, praised the unorthodox director for sticking to his old name:

Are we not approaching a saturation point in this delicate subject of hebraizing our names? Its roots, not always conscious, lie deep in the emotional foundation of the Zionist revolution. . . . I, for myself, think that the name of Ciechanover is beautiful, authentic, indigenous and historical, unlike Ron, Gil, On, and other Sabra names emerging out of the psychological depths nourished by the state's childhood illnesses.[24]

Indeed, the whole attitude of the galut Jews began to undergo a deep change. Were not the real heroes of the Yishuv Diaspora Jews? Who were the leaders of the pre-state undergrounds if not ex-yeshiva youngsters who brought with them the very courage and determination whose absence is allegedly the characteristic of the "inferior step-brother"? And did not two million Diaspora Jews fight in the Allied Armies in World War II? Did not volunteers from the Diaspora fight in Palestine as part of the British Jewish Legion during World War I and as courageous volunteers in the war of Israel's independence?

Finally, was not the accusation leveled against Europe's dead Jews for passively going to the slaughterhouse a case of moral insanity? As the Holocaust receded into painful memory, the axioms of Sabra smugness were re-examined and gave way to a recognition of the harsh facts. The reality was that millions of non-Jews passively subjected themselves to Nazi terror and that Jews alone dared organize in the doomed ghettoes of Poland an armed rebellion of the starving few against the might of the Third Reich. Hundreds of thousands of Russian prisoners of war, wantonly massacred and starved to death by the Wehrmacht, did not raise a hand against their German persecutors. And what could the Jews, helplessly alone and fragmented in the midst of Nazi-dominated Europe and surrounded by an anti-Semitic population, achieve by staging revolts against the omnipotent death machine? They certainly could not save themselves or postpone their death through such desperate acts.

In Sabra legend, their passivity was a blemish on their honor. But what honor was involved? There were no war rules in the confrontation between the doomed Jews and Nazi barbarity. In the face of German brutality, all codes of human behavior vanished; the one ethical commandment was survival in the hope that the defeat of the Nazis would precede total extinction. The courage of the few who decided to die, arms in hand, rather than submit to the further humiliation by the Nazis is justly regarded as one of the most heroic chapters in human history. But can these rebellions, a conscious decision to commit suicide, cast a stone at the helpless, dispersed, Jewish communities, constantly deceived by the Nazis, betrayed by the Allies, hoping that the worst rumors were baseless and that they would manage to survive the next wave of convoys to the concentration camps?

These questions could not but deeply trouble thinking Sabras who were gradually waking from their euphoric self-indulgence. They were brought up to believe that "honor" required the Jews to act as the new Hebrews expected them to. But as the study of the Holocaust deepened and extended they realized that this truism crumbled in the face of accumulated facts. The Yishuv's attitude to the massacred Jews of Europe expressed itself in one heroic act: In 1944, young men and women, sent by the Yishuv's leaders, parachuted into Europe to assist the remaining shrunken Jewish communities. This exceptional mission—the only direct help reaching the Jews from the outside world throughout the Holocaust—has been justly glorified and seen as the personification of the new Hebrew character. The bravery and dedication of the parachutists symbolize the determination to put an end to Jewish passivity, to defy danger and to die, if need be, in the battle against the enemy. Together with the Jewish Brigade, fighting with the

Allies, and the Jewish underground in Palestine, these volunteers are enshrined in the national memory of Israelis and their deeds have become part of the country's proudest heritage.

Yet, the parachutists failed to carry out their mission to organize an armed resistance of the remaining Jews and actively oppose the Nazis. Nowhere did they attain an operational capacity. In Hungary, they were caught by the authorities, and two, including the legendary Hannah Senesh, were executed. In Yugoslavia, Italy, Rumania, and Bulgaria, they were, for various reasons, prevented from organizing a Jewish opposition. Only in Slovakia did they manage to reach a center of a revolt against the Nazis, and there organize the reluctant Jews into a fighting unit. When the Nazis ruthlessly stamped out the rebellion, the Jews, led by the young Palestinians, sought sanctuary in the mountains from which they were supposed to continue their armed struggle. They were soon discovered by the Germans and annihilated.

The heroic attempt ended in catastrophe. Only a handful were saved to tell the horrific tale—a tale of strong opposition to the parachutists' plans. One of the local Zionist leaders addressed the dedicated three men and one woman who dropped out of the sky from distant Palestine in words whose shattering impact remains undiminished to this day:

Actually, for what purpose did you come here? What did you think, that this was a child's game here? You wanted to be heroes? Spies? What for? I know what you will say: You want to help, to represent the Yishuv in Eretz Israel. You will tell me stories about conscience and solidarity. . . . Rubbish! Nonsense! Who called for you? Who needs you? . . . You came here to play soldiers. . . . You are proud and rave about your upstanding fearlessness, as if you came to us here as representatives of some sort of super Eretz Israeli race. Well, know you: We are not ashamed to hide, to grovel, to run, to steal through borders—because we want to save one more Jew and another Jew from this graveyard.[25]

In his book, *Post Ugandan Zionism in the Crucible of the Holocaust*, S. B. Beit Zvi comments on this episode:

The words about a "sort of super Eretz Israeli race" were not ground-less. The psychological background to the despatch of the parachut-ists stemmed from the belief then current in the Yishuv that the Jews of Eretz Israel, or at least the young pioneers among them, were distin-guished by their excellent qualities from the galut Jews. Based upon this belief, it was possible to assume that a handful of parachutists would instruct the local Jews how to act and what to do.[26]

Such a reappraisal of what constituted heroism and honor in the Holocaust cast a new light on the basic foundations of the Sabra's outlook. His very superiority, in time of utmost crisis, was being questioned. The traditional Jewish instincts—to flee, to run, to kowtow if need be, to survive—proved perhaps more honorable, in the true sense of the word, than the acts of heroism which he grew up to admire.

But the doubts run even deeper. What would have happened to the proud Hebrew Yishuv had Rommel's troops not been stopped at the gates of Alexandria? Had Palestine been over-taken by the Huns, how would the new Jews have fared? The Jewish underground had its plans for resistance, but given the overwhelming superiority of the Nazis and their experience in crushing opposition, it is safe to assume that the Jewish resis-tance in Palestine would have come to nought. Within a short period of time, the Nazi death machine, with the gleeful assis-tance of many Palestinian Arabs, whose Grand Mufti sat in Berlin spreading his own brand of Jew-hatred, would have be-gun its process of total annihilation of the Palestinian Jews. Because of their relatively small number—600,000 Jews—their concentration in small areas, and the active enmity of the Arab majority, liquidation of the Yishuv would have been a rela-tively simple affair. As a matter of fact, the Germans planned such an extermination, aided and abetted by Nazi Arabs and Palestinian Germans, sons of the Templar settlers, who joined the Nazi party in Palestine in the 1930s.

The ramifications of such a hypothetical turn of events could not escape the newly awakened consciousness of young Israe-lis and their effect on the traditional image of the new Jew can be surmised. Seen in this light, the Holocaust, far from reaffirming the dichotomy between old inferior Jews and new superior Hebrews, erased prior Zionist distinctions between the two branches of a menaced Jewry.

The Sabra reappraisal of his Jewish past did not produce a massive return to Judaism. On the contrary, the great majority of young Israelis are as secular as ever. But one manifestation attests to the depth of the new mood: Out of the Sabra generation arose, in the late sixties and seventies, a movement of *Hozrim b'teshuvah*, of repentants, or "born again" Jews. The movement became significant not only because it reversed the regular Israeli trend of moving away from religion but mainly because it involved a large number of classic, secular Sabras, among them famous artists and entertainers. These were not content with a flight into the yeshiva but insisted on joining the most Orthodox and reclusive segments in the religious community. Their act became symbolic: Out of the cafés of Dizengoff Street, out of the most permissive circles of Sabra environment, they crossed over to a society barely associated with Israel, resembling, as it does, the ghetto-like shtetl existence. The typical Sabra was transformed into the galut image of his forefather. The Sabra grandson took over the shape of his grandfather, that very grandfather against whom his father had staged his Zionist rebellion. In one case, this transition acquired nationwide visibility. Uri Zohar, an entertainer and actor, had been for many years synonymous with Sabra humor and folklore. With Dahn Ben Amotz, he created a whole language of Sabra quips and aphorisms. His very appearance on television, where he had his own show, bespoke Sabraness. Then, in front of his admiring audience, Uri Zohar—again, the unmistakable Sabra name—changed his persona. The Sabra hero was transformed into an Orthodox Jew: first the skullcap, then the side-curls, finally the beard and bearing of an Orthodox grandfatherly person. After he left public life and television, Uri Zohar completed this metamorphosis from sandal-shod native son to heavily garmented, bent shtetl chasid.

Occasionally, these Sabras-turned-chasidim join the most militant Orthodox groups of the Mea Shearim quarter in Jerusalem, from which they emerge to throw stones at cars traveling on the Sabbath. From the heartland of Israel they have traversed all the way to the non-Zionist shelters of galut within Israel. Just as their fathers ran from Jewish isolation, seeking participation in current history and culture, so do these Sabra sons seek refuge from current history in a haven where Judaism, unaltered by the outside world, reigns eternal.

This extreme manifestation of a Sabra identity crisis—admittedly involving a small but conspicuous minority—stems not only from individual problems or from a worldwide disenchantment with secular values. Behind it lies a national crisis. The Sabra, born and educated to regard himself as superior to Diaspora Jews, woke one day to realize that the classical galut type is gone and that today's western and American Jews hardly fit the mold of yesteryear. The Jewish communities of North America cannot be conceived as the "inferior step brothers." On the contrary, they are wealthy, proud, self-assured, sophisticated, and financially and politically helpful to Israel. In times of need, and especially since the Yom Kippur War, Israel turns to them in the same way that menaced Jewish communities turned to their stronger brethren in the West. Here, too, the roles are seen as a reversal of the original Herzlian dream. In Zionist philosophy, the creation of a Jewish state eliminated the Diaspora: Those who do not immigrate to the Jewish state assimilate into the host nations. In present-day Zionism, we see the creation of a new Diaspora, that of the Israeli *yordim*, the Sabra emigrés who form their own Jewish communities in America—from New York to Los Angeles.

All these occurrences, reversing the very ethos on which Sabras grew up, were bound to have the deepest impact on the national psyche. Normalcy was supposed to have culminated in the Sabra nation, but things did not work out that way. Indicative is a poll conducted among Israeli kindergarten children. Asked "who are greater athletes, Israeli or galut Jews?"

the children instinctively replied that the Israelis, of course, were the top men. When queried about Mark Spitz and other famous American Jewish athletes, the kids responded that they did not have these sportsmen in mind. Why? "America is not galut; galut is Poland. That's why."

9

A HOUSE DIVIDED

Is it at all possible to argue rationally with the new religious-nationalist mood which began to pervade Israel after the Six-Day War? Is any attempt to disprove the "holiness" of military conquests worth while? Is it profitable to seek and prove that there is no "eternal enmity" between Israel and "the goyim"? Inevitably such a debate will be less than fruitful. Suffice it to say that even within the religious camp—both outside and inside Israel—Gush Emunim's doctrine is heatedly rejected and the combination of messianism with nationalism, Halachah with armed might, is rejected as a perverted interpretation of Jewish tradition. Rabbi Shmuel Rabinovitz, son of England's chief rabbi, summed up this rejection by branding it a type of Jewish fanaticism and blaming it for both misrepresenting true Judaism and constituting a veritable danger to Israel's future.[1] Others point out that the Jewish people lost their independence in self-willed and hopeless conflicts with the Roman Empire, unnecessary conflicts which were brought about by the kind of zealotry represented today by Gush extremists. Indeed, the specter of a divided house haunts the Israeli mind, reviving images of Second Temple Jerusalem under siege, with the zealots seeking to exacerbate the conflict, rejecting all compromise, terrorizing the moderates and, above all, believing that theirs is the only way to salvation.

A discussion of Israel's predicament is therefore productive only if it is couched in rational terms. In such terms, one phenomenon looms over all other issues in present day Israel: the assumption that Israel is—contrary to all Zionist aspirations—

the successor to, and inheritor of, the rejected Jew, and consequently, whatever Israel does, it is doomed to be a lonely nation. In its secular version, this fate is often seen as an inevitable curse which Israel would like to, but cannot, escape. To the extremist religious camp, this lot corroborates ancient truisms and confirms the historical continuity of Jewish history: In a world where the Arabs are the successors of the Jebusites and Amalekites, Israel's aloneness is seen as a blessing in disguise.

Yet, when one examines the factual foundations of this mood, it is somewhat difficult to understand its prevalence. In modern history there seems to be no analogous case where one nation succeeded in enlisting the goodwill and support of so many other nations. Throughout its short history, Israel could count on such support—both moral and economic. The figures for foreign aid received by Israel from the United States are staggering: From 1973 to 1983 Israel, as the recipient of American aid, in one form or another, totalling over twenty-five billion dollars, stands first in the list of beneficiaries of American generosity, a position which should have refuted all the gibberish about "the whole world is against us." At different junctures of its precarious existence—in the 1948 war, in the aftermath of the Yom Kippur debacle—Israel received a helping hand without which its capacity to stand against the Arabs would have been greatly jeopardized. Indeed, one of the most paradoxical chapters in this sad story is the effect of the Six-Day War itself. This watershed event played a crucial role in creating a new consciousness of Israel's isolation, feeding as it did the new nationalism with the specter of a solitary Israel facing the Arab threat to accomplish the destruction Hitler failed to complete.

But the truth of the matter is rather different. In her hour of trial, Israel was not alone. On the contrary, one can hardly recall a similar moment in history when one small nation, with little to offer the world other than its social and cultural achievements, enlisted such total support as Israel did before, during, and immediately after that war. Wherever people could express their feelings, there was an overwhelming anxiety preceding the war and a joyous sigh of relief when it ended in Israel's swift victory. It is seen in the world press of those days: a total support in the editorial pages as well as news reports of mass demonstrations, petitions, contributions—all testifying to an unprecedented mobilization for the cause of the menaced Jewish state. Thousands of volunteers were ready to come and help and in pro-Israel rallies leaders of all political persuasions—including not a few Eurocommunists—took part.

When victory came, a tidal wave of identification with Israel swept over the free world, and so strong was its emotional impact that it spilled over the iron curtain into East European bloc countries, where open defiance of the official anti-Israeli policy was quite common. The reaction of the world press was so overtly pro-Israel—*Time*'s essay "Arabia Decepta" springs to mind as one of many instances—that it worried western diplomats in Arab capitals and forced Arab propagandists to radically alter their public stand vis-à-vis the Jewish state. Indeed, one cannot think of a parallel case, including that of Republican Spain fighting for its life, in which the free press was united in its support of one side to a local war.

How then can one explain the fact that the very event which rallied "the world" behind menaced Israel was seen by so many Israelis as the crucial turning point ushering in a new isolationist view? The explanation lies in the inability of many Israelis to see their political predicament with realistic eyes. Israel's dilemma has always been one of realpolitik. Because of the Moslem-Arab rejection of its very existence and because of the political and economic prowess of the Arabs, other nations' self-interest tends to tilt against the Jewish state. There is no permanent, long-range interest in forming a binding and formal alliance with Israel, when such an alliance is bound to bring upon it the wrath of a rich and powerful bloc. Thus, in a world of growing regional cooperation and military alliances, Israel is

a solitary exception of political loneliness. Ben Gurion, understanding this basic predicament, formulated a policy based
upon Israel's moral claim, as well as on a series of short-range,
temporary, and informal pacts, such as those with the Soviet
bloc, which supplied the fledging state with vital arms denied
to it by the West during the War of Independence and with
France and England in the mid-fifties during the Suez crisis.
Israel's special position in the United States is also based on a
mixture of moral obligations and a grudging recognition that in
the shifting sands of the Middle East Israel is a solid anti-Soviet
base. But the hard facts which govern Israel's international
posture dictate an ambivalent attitude toward it: The instinctive sympathy clashes with self-interest, and sentiment is con-
tradicted by politics.

This duality was demonstrated in those anxious days preceding the Six-Day War. Israel was left alone—politically and mili-
tarily—to face what was then seen as a life-or-death struggle,
but its cause was championed by free men everywhere. To fail
to realize this duality is to fail to grasp the very facts of international life. To draw an analogy between Israel's *political* aloneness and the tragic fate of the Jewish community in Europe (as
ex-Prime Minister Begin often did with his customary fire and
brimstone speeches) is to turn a blind eye to the world in
which we live. Staunch anti-Israeli stands are now the daily
fodder of Third World arenas where Israel is habitually branded
together with South Africa as the moral lepers of mankind.
Yet, Third World countries have no anti-Semitic tradition and
to ascribe to them an anti-Jewish sentiment means to decree
an eternal conflict between the Jewish state and everybody
else, thus flying in the face of facts: Israel's unique achievements in Africa withstood the test of the 1967 war and began
to deteriorate only after the African states could not persuade
Israel to adopt a more flexible line toward a possible settlement
with Egypt. When one contrasts this with what began to take
place in Israel after 1967, one must suspect that the transition
from deep anxiety to victorious delirium has somewhat ob-

scured Israel's vision of the world and the harsh realities it must learn to accept.

This unrealistic vision has, alas, become self-fulfilling. Since the Six-Day War, Israeli governments have been implementing a national policy which runs counter to international consensus and to the very political philosophy espoused by the diminishing circle of Israel's friends. The West Bank is seen not as a bargaining card for an eventual peace but as grounds for Israeli settlements and creeping annexation. Since the 1967 war, the Palestinian Arabs have been subject to military occupation and shorn of most of their political rights. Israel embarked upon a collision course with its traditional supporters and allies. Thus "the world" really began to be "against us" and this was seen by anxious Israelis as further proof of their darkest suspicions. What began as a reckless mood of triumphant exhilaration ends as a fulfilled prophecy. Peace with Egypt seemed originally to change the course of events. Israel proved, in deed and word, that when given a partner, its readiness to make concessions in return for peace was virtually unlimited. But the rejection of the Camp David accords by the Palestinians and by the Arab world, coupled with Israel's insistence on changing the status quo in the West Bank through intensive settlement and creating "facts," belittled the impact of peace with Egypt. With tension growing in the West Bank, with the trauma of war in Lebanon and its aftermath, Israel has been dragged, even before the peace with Egypt had a chance to be tested, into the familiar pattern: Her actions, seen at home by the government as justifiable self-defense, are decried by a world whose duplicity and double-standards are seen by many Israelis as further evidence of their "aloneness."

Thus Israel's predicament is governed, primarily by its inferior political status in an international arena where she is pitched against an economically superior Arab front. The fallout from this confrontation on Israel's relations with the outside world, exacerbated by a domestic policy colliding with an international consensus, has created within Israel a singular

climate conducive to the analogy between the pariah people
and the pariah state.

On the validity of this analogy hangs the future of the Jewish
state. Indeed, it may be said that for Israel there is only one
philosophical question: Is its failure to gain acceptance in the
Middle East inherently and inevitably connected with the historical failure of the Jews to gain acceptance in gentile society,
or are the two rejections inherently different? Are we witnessing two manifestations of the same historical phenomenon, or
are we dealing with two separate, accidentally similar, historical chapters?

That the analogy is drawn in the first place attests to the
depths of the crisis engulfing present-day Israel. But upon
closer examination, the analogy itself appears to rest on false
assumptions. The Arab rejection of Israel is familiar. They regard the whole of Palestine as Arab land and their clash with
Zionism and Israel is that of two national movements fighting
over the same piece of land. The resort to traditional Islamic,
as well as to western European, anti-Semitism is instrumental;
it serves the national purpose of returning Palestine to its
"Arab owners." Furthermore, while Israel rightly sees itself as
an asylum island, constantly in danger of being engulfed by the
armed hatred surrounding it, Arabs have convinced themselves
that Israel is the brute force which is responsible for the plight
of the Palestinian refugees, rules over a despondent Arab minority within its territory, and whose air force can wreak havoc
from Beirut to Baghdad. To foreign eyes, Israel's armed might
and military reprisals seem as far removed from the traditional
passivity of the persecuted Jewish community as conceivably
possible. Occasionally, some observers go further and errone-
ously compare the dispossessed Palestinians of today with the
Jews of yesteryear, thus creating a role reversal between Arab
and Jew. The analogy is erroneous, but the fact remains that
Israel is fighting a war, with all the attendant cruelty and injustice, while Jews in Exile suffered without being able to defend
themselves against cruelty and injustice.

The two rejections differ in a fundamental way. From fifteenth-century Spain to Nazi Germany, traditional anti-Semitism has been characterized by an irrational element bordering on insanity. Christian societies were ready to sacrifice economic and social advantages and self-interest for the sake of that "sacred" duty to punish the sinful race. One does not have to subscribe to contemporary German author Sebastian Hafner's theory or to Professor Yehuda Bauer's observations ascribing all of Hitler's moves, including his readiness to sacrifice Germany itself, to his demonic determination to exterminate the Jews in order to realize this. Admittedly, the Nazi model is a case of a deranged regime; yet, traditional anti-Semitism has always been imbued with a kernel of insanity: The Jews who served their host societies with their talents and devotion were expelled and ostracized, portrayed as the embodiment of Satan, accused of ritual murders, depicted simultaneously as the representatives of both international capitalism and subversive communism.

At the heart of Israel's relations with the outside world there lies no such madness. The opposite is true: Rational considerations of self-interest militate against siding with Israel because the balance of cost and benefit tilts against her. Israel often gains support in spite of this cold calculation when passion and sentiment overcome utilitarian considerations. Indeed, Israel has sought and received support in the name of a prodemocratic sentiment as against considerations of realpolitik. There is, therefore, an ideological chasm between traditional anti-Semitism, spurning reason and self-interest, and the isolation which plagues Israel, stemming as it does from reasons of selfish expedience.

But, above all, there looms another factor—theoretical as well as practical—which distinguishes between the two rejections. Anti-Semitism in its varied forms was aimed against a people who, despite their dispersion, have kept their religious, cultural, and national ties in a way unknown elsewhere in the annals of history. Like two primeval elements embraced in an

---

eternal conflict, so have these two universal phenomena of survival and persecution persisted to the point that they seem to have acquired a transcendent dimension which exceeds and nullifies the rules of history. By the time part of Christian civilization had been ready to grant Jews equal status, it was already too late. European society, despite its secular elements, could not rid itself of the ingrained prejudice and demanded that the Jews lose any shred of self-identity and all "tribal" affinities. Jews, too, could not eradicate the residue of their age-long inferiority, of everything which life in exile has imprinted in their psyche; they could not, or would not, totally assimilate into societies which could not, or would not, absorb them. Where such mutual acceptance reached its highest point, in post-emancipation Germany, the age-long hatred reached diabolical depths. Jewish-Gentile relations in the Diaspora suffer, ipso facto, from subliminal layers of history; or, as some would have it, from metahistorical elements whose roots reach to time immemorial and cannot be explained through rational arguments.

Such residual experiences do not color Israel's relations with the world around it. The international hardships that it encounters are by their very nature political, short-ranged, and devoid of historical roots. They disappear when the source of friction vanishes. Just as the hatred of the Jews is fathomless, Israel's rejection is shallow. When, as in the case of the initial peace honeymoon with Egypt, it seemed that all political obstacles had been removed, the whole accompanying animosity was drained away with a swiftness that one has learned to expect from similar conflict-situations elsewhere. In vain does Gush Emunim seek to find contradictory proof, but not in vain do they invoke the alleged perpetual nature of the conflict between Jews and the world around them as a self-evident truism.

In order to demonstrate the inherent difference between the pre-Zionist Jewish predicament and Israel's "normal" difficulties, one may resort to the following hypothetical exercise:

In a miraculous way, Israel succeeds in removing itself from the Middle East; a cosmic knife cuts her loose, unlodges and carries her as an island to midocean. Israel conducts her national life away from the constant friction with her Arab neighbors. Would it be conceivable, in such circumstances, to imagine a perpetual conflict between the Jewish state and "the world"? Would it be possible to employ then the customary language about a "Jewish fate" which ostracizes the Jew wherever he lives, in exile or in his own state? Would not such physical disengagement from the Arab world put an end to all that emotional mumbo jumbo with which Israelis clothe their current difficulties?

The conclusion must be that Israel's troubles are not at all of the kind which have plagued, and still continue to plague, Jews as minorities in reluctant host societies. Israel's troubles stem from geopolitical circumstances which have nothing to do with the religious, historical, and psychological obsessions which have accompanied the dispersed Jews. To hold otherwise is not only to negate the very raison d'être of Israel but to fly in the face of fact.

It is, however, always legitimate to claim that beyond these facts and the geopolitical circumstances, there lies, unseen, a mysterious scheme, underlying the tragedy of the Arab-Jewish conflict and the consequent friction with the outside world, which cannot be understood by ordinary rules of history. One may argue that the failure of the Jews to assimilate into their surroundings—a failure that had accompanied them like a plague or a blessing from the days of the Patriarchs—is responsible for the rejection of Israel by the Arab world. One may also contend that behind the political decisions made by Israel since the 1967 war, there stands a subconscious will to cling to a sense of Jewish uniqueness which, although lacking a religious underpinning, must reflect such a preordained scheme. One may, as many Israeli secular men of letters have recently done, invoke the eternity of Israel—the fate of the people, as distinct from the transitory existence of Israel the State. All these ponderings and gnawing doubts are not new. Ahad

Ha'am, the great rationalist who clothed the complex history of the Jews with a totally national interpretation, had his moments of doubts and wondered aloud whether rational tools were adequate to explain the perplexing role which Jews have played on mankind's stage:

History has not yet satisfactorily explained how it came about that a tiny nation in a corner of Asia produced a unique religious ethical outlook, which, though it has had so profound an influence on the rest of the world, has yet remained so foreign to the rest of the world, and to this day has been unable either to master it or to be mastered by it. This is a historical phenomenon to which, despite many attempted answers, we must still attach a note of interrogation. But every true Jew, be he Orthodox or liberal, feels in the depths of his being that there is something in the spirit of our people—though we do not know what it is—which has prevented us from following the rest of the world along the beaten path, has led to our producing this Judaism of ours, and has kept us and our Judaism "in a corner" to this day, because we cannot abandon the distinctive outlook on which Judaism is based.[2]

Such sentiments, though vulgarized by many Israelis into facile phrases and metaphysical gibberish, are not incompatible with the Zionist yearning to reverse the course of Jewish history. Yet speculations about a meta-historical dimension not dreamed of in our philosophy cannot be a useful guide to the preservation and survival of Israel. Moreover, when such sentiments are uttered by totally secular Israelis, one immediately suspects that they are seeking to evade real dilemmas by paying easy lip-service to the mysterious element in Judaism without accepting its obligatory commandments. Are we not facing, in such instances, a more refined version of the secular Israeli who does not believe in God but reiterates that God promised him the whole of the Land of Israel?

Furthermore, invoking Jewish history in order to support a deterministic view is a double-edged sword. The great similarity, often stressed by this school of thought, between Second Temple Jerusalem and present-day Israel must not necessarily be taken as a case for the power of predestination. On the contrary, if a historical lesson can be elicited at all from such an analogy, it is one that militates against extremism, against irrationality, against an attempt to provoke an uneven contest between Jerusalem and "the world." Seen retrospectively, the heroic figures of the revolt against Rome, who were ready to sacrifice the very existence of a Jewish community in its homeland, to induce a fratricidal civil war, provoke the mighty Roman legions into unnecessary bloodshed, were responsible for bringing about the greatest calamity in Jewish history.

Occasionally, such a juxtaposition between past and present can acquire dramatic impact. In the summer of 1981, the Khan Theater of Jerusalem presented a new Israeli play. Entitled *The Wars of the Jews* and written by Joshua Sobol, a supporter of Peace Now, it depicted with moving authenticity the debate within besieged Jerusalem before its final conquest and destruction at the hands of Titus's legions. It was staged in David's Citadel, where Herodian stones, witnesses to the fall of Jerusalem, peered at the audience below the Ottoman and Crusader superstructure. The audience was attentive, and some displayed barely concealed emotion or anger. The subject of the play was the war fought on that very site two thousand years ago: a handful of starved Jews bravely battling against the might of Rome. The play's hero is Rabbi Yohanan Ben Zakkai, the realist who refuses to be drawn into the suicidal war and steals away from the doomed city to Yavneh in order to establish a new place of learning, a temporary shelter in which Jewish thought could survive. The villains are the zealots, the fanatical freedom fighters who are ready to risk the precarious existence of the Jews in their land through a reckless provocation, bringing down upon them the wrath of the whole Roman world. Between the sanity of Rabbi Ben Zakkai and the paranoia of the zealots stand the moderates, the citizenry of Jerusalem. They realize the dangers involved in the approaching confrontation but they cannot stem or resist the emotional tide stirred up by the zealots. They seek to preserve national unity and political consensus in the face of the menace outside the beleaguered walls.

As the play ended, applause mingled with booing. The crowd thinned out and dispersed. Small circles of young spectators gathered and heatedly debated the contemporary lessons to be drawn from this ancient and living tale. Alongside the Citadel's walls a small group of Orthodox Jews, clad in their shtreimels and kapotas made their way through empty Arab alleys to a midnight vigil at the Wailing Wall.

10

THE ZIONIST DREAM REVISITED

Is Israel's destiny to be like other nations? Will it not only give expression to a different national character but also fulfill a unique role? Will it forever "reside alone"? When grappling with the problems outlined in this book, one cannot invoke an objective scientific approach.

In the final analysis, everything depends on axiomatic assumptions and on a basic philosophical attitude. Is one's attitude based on a religious premise, seeing Israel as the embodiment of a Divine promise, clothing it with sanctity, making it subservient to God's Laws? Is Israel's position among the nations dictated by that Divine commandment which set it apart from the "families of the earth?" Or is the primary premise a secular wish to preserve the Jewish people in their state and from this derives everything else—including the attitude toward Divine commandments? Should we regard religious tradition as merely one manifestation of a perpetual national entity which changes its garments with time and circumstance? Or should we go further and regard Israel not as a modern reincarnation of the old Jewish civilization but rather as the creation of a new nation which cast off its links with the old Jewish world, a satellite which has pried itself loose from the old launching pad—a butterfly, as it were, emerging from exile's cocoon?

These dilemmas, at the personal level, require a clear-cut attitudinal choice: total religious continuity; continuity in a modified national sense; nationality which severs past traditions. Philosophically, there can be no compromise between these different approaches, each ascribing a different raison d'être to Jewish survival. It is possible—perhaps, even necessary—to reach a political compromise between the contesting groups and parties within Israel in order to formulate some sort of national consensus. Given an inherent inadvisability of a national showdown and Israel's external difficulties, such a compromise is perhaps inevitable.

But in formulating one's personal attitude, such a compromise—a concoction combining a bit of Herzlian Zionism, spiced by messianic religiosity, with a smattering of neo-Canaanite thinking—is an exercise in intellectual dishonesty. Conceptually, one cannot bridge the inevitable gap between Herzl and his disciples, on the one hand, and the rabbis of Gush Emunim and their followers, on the other. The contradiction is fundamental because it relates to the very foundation of the Zionist idea. This does not mean that anyone subscribing to the original Zionist school and seeing Jewish history from a national point of view (in this respect there is little difference between Herzl and Ahad Ha'am, Jabotinsky and Ben Gurion) turns a blind eye to the role played by religious tradition or denies the glory of its continued survival as a cementing force in the life of the Jewish people. A national viewpoint does not necessarily involve an acceptance of the school which regards religion as merely one transient manifestation of a permanent national identity. There is something artificial and contrived about such an outlook when applied to a people whose very existence and survival in the past were inextricably linked with an extreme monotheism and the strict observance of laws and rules emanating from the Torah given to Moses on Mount Sinai.

Before the emancipation of the Jews in Europe, there could have been no doubt among Jews and non-Jews alike, that Jewish civilization, which preserved its very uniqueness in a way foreign to the "rules of history," is explicable only in terms of a communion of religious belief and ethnic affinity. The idea of an independently secular Jewish nation is of relatively recent origin, and to this day its primary concepts suffer from a cer-

tain ideological fogginess. But recognizing this historical process does not mean accepting a uniform and monolithic interpretation of Jewish history and of the forces motivating the
Jewish will to survive as a separate entity from its formative
period to the present day. Even if we recognize, as we definitely
should, the common religious bond which created in the past
the very definition of all things Jewish, we must understand
the radical shift which Jewish history has undergone in modern times. This shift took place once Jewish civilization lost,
under the impact of emancipation and attempted assimilation,
its monolithic nature. Once the walls of the ghetto caved in
under both internal and external pressures, once Jews began to
break out of these walls, they also severed that common bond
which lay at the heart of Jewish civilization. One often uses
the term "Zionist revolution" because it charted a new course
and articulated a new definition of existence for the Jews.
"Revolutionary" is indeed an apt term in many respects. While
Zionism sought to keep a sense of historical continuity, it
nevertheless defined anew the basic assumptions of Jewish civilization, decreeing that it is governed no longer by a common
faith but by a common national will.

However, it was not Zionism which created the break with
the past. On the contrary, when the Lovers of Zion appeared
in Eastern Europe and Herzl began to dream an impossible
dream in the West, Jewish civilization had already been
shaken and splintered. Emancipation in the West and promises of a new era in the East had opened up to Jews previously locked gates. The vigor and forcefulness with which
Jews stormed these gates, even when left only slightly ajar,
the speed with which they were ready to shed their old habits
and adapt even their religious tradition to the non-Jewish
world, were witnesses to the state of the old ramparts. In
Eastern Europe, even within the Pale of Settlement, where the
majority of Yiddish-speaking Jews clung to the old ways, the
sweeping unrest began to shake the community. There, too,
the unrest found its first expression in a demand for emanci-

pation—even at the price of Russification and a surprising willingness to be absorbed into Mother Russia—and only later, when that demand met a wall of rejection, that unrest found its alternative revolutionary channel. When Zionism appeared on stage, it sought to save the Jewish world from a total loss of self-identity. Thus, in the wake of Emancipation—real as well as attempted—a new brand of Jewishness grew which both shirked the yoke of tradition and spurned the lure of assimilation.

Side by side with Zionism, an emigration movement which began as a thin trickle at the turn of the century developed into a mighty stream and grew into a flood, as millions of Jews from Eastern Europe reached the safe shores of the New World. In its own way, this massive movement, having no ideological motive outside the traditional Jewish instinct to flee an affliction and find a haven, testified to the depths of the crisis of tradition. The Jews flocked to the big cities of America and quickly established their own environments and communities. Nevertheless, traditional Orthodoxy could not maintain its hold in a new emancipated society and became the domain of a minority. It lost its former position of leadership to other groups eager to embrace the American ethos of a melting pot, equality of all races, and inter-religious ecumenicalism. The very essence of this American ethos contradicts the traditional Jewish emphasis on exclusivity and uniqueness. This emphasis, which could thrive under the cloudy skies of the Pale of Settlement, wilted under an American sun radiating enough equality to enable Jews to escape both persecution and the shackles of an antiquated doctrine. In other words, when we claim that Emancipation created a rift in the history of the Jewish people and rescinded for most of the Jews many of the old tenets we merely describe what happens to most Jews wherever given the opportunity to break loose from old bonds.

It is evident that there is a clear distinction between two eras of Jewish history—before and after Emancipation. In the first era, despite their dispersal and the lack of a homeland,

Jews kept their devotion to the laws and customs of their faith in a way that can only arouse astonishment and admiration. In the second era, this common denominator lost its binding power and a new reality took its place, in which a vague sense of tradition and communal affinity replaced strict observance, pluralism was substituted for uniformity and nationalism superseded messianic longings. This rift in history was not only a fact but also a juncture which created—if one may borrow a term from jurisprudence—a new basic norm. Before Emancipation every rule of behavior emanated from, or was ascribed to, Mosaic Law; the new basic norm was a national will to survive.

This transition clarifies why the centrality of Israel is so vital a postulate for Jewish survival. In the pre-emancipation era, no territorial homeland was needed because insulated Judaism was universal, independent of any national allegiance and existed wherever Jews could form a vital community. But a Judaism which is pluralistic, semisecular, exposed to external influences, unshielded from the vagaries of modernity could no longer survive without a homeland as a focal point of both pride and allegiance.

It is on this issue that the battle is joined within Israel. Gush Emunim and its followers among the new religious Right give a fundamentalist answer to Jewish dilemmas, overlooking the rift created by modernity. Their simplistic convictions, which appeal to so many Israelis because of this very quality, avoid the issues presented not only by the world today but also by the very nature of contemporary Jewish society.

But religious chauvinism in Israel also ignores problems created within a strict Orthodox tradition. Their attitude to the non-Jew, both within and outside Israel, invokes sayings and rules from the Halachah which date back to the very origins of Judaic law. Theirs, so they claim, is the true interpretation governing relations between the People of the Covenant and the rest of the world. Their interpretation of Mosaic sources is rejected by many religious sages and thinkers within

Israel and, needless to say, finds no receptive ears in non-Orthodox Jewish communities in the Diaspora. But the very issue which they have raised should be examined and exposed to a frank discussion.

Judaism was forged in a desperate battle against paganism; it was an island of monotheism in an idol-worshipping civilization. The central themes of Mosaic Law and biblical admonitions—chosenness, sanctity, the Covenant—were the issues on which this battle was joined. By the time other monotheistic creeds came into being, the Jews had lost their independence and were fragmented into subservient minorities living, at best, on sufferance of others and always subject to intermittent persecution. Jewish laws pertaining to the pagans, the worshippers of idols, were thus instinctively applied to the new oppressors—Christians as well as Moslems—with an understandable vengeance. This application served a dual function: preserving the separate entity of the endangered creed and providing a kind of psychological relief from, and a sublimated retribution for, the humiliation and suffering inflicted upon them. As the persecution of the Jews in the Middle Ages grew to horrific proportions, so did the anti-gentile streak acquire a more explicit, if merely academic, nature. There had always been theological elements justifying such an attitude, but the growth of persecution drenched these elements in blood and the fires of the Inquisition charred them beyond recognition. How pathetic was this Jewish response to the blood libels, the stakes, and the pogroms.

The Jews scribbled on papers their claim to superiority, corroborating in the rabbinical responsa the inferior nature of the heathen non-Jew, elaborating on his state of rightlessness, adumbrating the injunctions against lending him assistance or credibility. While they scribbled these impotent dicta, Jews were being expelled, burned at the stake, beaten to death, and massacred en masse. In this uneven contest, Christian anti-Semitism scourged the Jews with physical violence while the Jews had to contend themselves with a paper revenge, inveigh-

ing against the Gentiles with their Talmudic scholarism, drawing a direct analogy between the Christians and the idolators
against whom the Prophets rained their fury. Until the Age of
Enlightenment, the Jews had virtually no legal rights in Christian Europe, but in their literature they denied such rights, in
their powerless rabbinical courts, to gentile witnesses.

That this paper vehemence against the non-Jew was directly
related to the state of the Jews cannot be doubted. Theological
considerations were influenced not only by dogma—which by
its very nature lends itself to various interpretations—but by
the actual relations between Jew and non-Jew. Professor Jacob
Katz of the Hebrew University, in a series of studies, demonstrated this link between the factual position of the Jewish
communities and their scholastic attitude to the Christians.
From the Middle Ages, when the very act of *kiddush hashem*,
the voluntary sacrifice of the Jewish martyrs, sought to demonstrate the moral superiority of their faith over their oppressors,
Jewish religious writings moved to an intermediate stage in the
sixteenth and seventeenth centuries: The Christian neighbor
acquired a new status and the common basis of Judaism and
Christianity was gradually admitted. The new Christian tolerance in the seventeenth and eighteenth centuries gave rise to a
new type of enlightened Jew, the Maskil, but its impact was not
lost even on the Orthodox rabbis. Two of the most renowned
sages of the time, Rabbi Yair Chaim Bachrach (1638–1702) and
Rabbi Yaacov Emden (1697–1776) reacted to the new tolerance
by emphasizing the common religious tradition of the two great
monotheistic creeds and the latter went even further by claiming that Jesus did not intend to deny the binding power of the
Torah but only aspired to spread the basic tenets of Judaism
among the Gentiles. The brutal conflict between Christians and
Jews was thus seen as but the tragic outcome of a historical
misunderstanding. With the rise of rationalism, this trend acquired greater influence—especially in such tolerant countries
as Germany, France, and Holland—and became manifest in the
humanistic and universalist approach of Moses Mendelssohn,

and later, of the founders of Reform Judaism. By 1807, when
Napoleon convened the famous Sanhedrin, a council of Jewish
scholars and sages from France, Italy, and Germany, to respond
to his questions about the nature of Judaism, the Jewish consensus had shifted toward an emphasis on the universalist nature of
the Jewish tradition and on the commandment to treat the
Christian citizens with brotherly love. The members of the
Napoleonic Sanhedrin wrote:

> This sentiment was at first aroused in us by the mere grant of tolera-
> tion. It has been increased, these eighteen years, by the Government's
> new favors to such a degree that now our fate is irrevocably united
> with the common fate of all Frenchmen. . . . It is impossible that a Jew
> should treat a Frenchman, not of his religion, in any other manner
> than he would treat one of his Israelitish brethren.[1]

Indeed, by the end of the nineteenth century, western Jewry
was so engrossed in this new ecumenical spirit, that many of
them were appalled by the tauntings of the new anti-Semites
citing, as they did, the embarrassing old quotations from forgotten pre-Emancipation days.

The reaction of the early Zionists to these old allegations of
the new anti-Semites was to cut through this maze of accusations, apologetic rebuttals, and counteraccusations and to turn
their backs on the two history-laden traditions. The Zionist
response was forthright: Their wish was to transplant the
newly born Jewish concept of true equality to all races from the
alien soil of Christian Europe to the promising land of Israel.
There, in Zion, will the new tolerance really thrive because the
Jews, having been the victims of prejudice and bigotry, will
create a new political climate, a true enlightened environment,
where the non-Jews will enjoy the rights that Jews sought in
vain. The new land—Herzl's *Altneuland* is merely one instance of this aspiration—is therefore the utopian mirror-image of the Christian society which the Jews desired. The Jews,
having gained their sovereignty, will do unto others what they
wanted others to do unto them.

This mirror-image concept dominates much of early Zionist literature and fills many pages in Herzl's utopia. Herzl is not blind to the dangers of a new Jewish chauvinism. In *Altneuland* this mirror-image anti-Semitism is personified by a character named Geyer, who appeals to the mob by flaunting his anti-gentile slogans. But Herzl inveighs against such views:

Hold fast to the things that have made us great: to liberality, tolerance, love of mankind. Only then is Zion truly Zion. . . . We stand and fall by the principle that whoever has given two years' service to the New Society as prescribed by our rules, and has conducted himself properly, is eligible to membership no matter what his race or creed.[2]

To Herzl, who named his Zionist periodical not *Zion* but *Die Welt*, it was clear that Geyer's anti-gentile view would be soundly defeated by the enlightened Jewish majority.

A delightful little utopia, written in 1898 by an Algerian Jew, Jacques Behar, made the same point through a grotesque parable. Entitled "Anti-Gentileness in Zion," the short tale appeared in *Die Welt*, while the Dreyfus affair was raging and its ramifications reached the shores of North Africa. Behar, who represented the Algerian Jews in the First Zionist Congress and depicted there the plight of his brethren, described in his piece the Jewish State in 1997, the one-hundredth anniversary of the Basel Congress.

In that year, the Jewish state witnesses an inverted Dreyfus case. A Jew is brought to trial because of an anti-gentile article he published in which he inveighs against the plots hatched by foreigners and non-Jews. The trial is a Dreyfus mirror-image except for one aspect: "while in Europe, the masses side with the bigots . . . the inhabitants of Jerusalem demonstrated the hatred they felt for him . . . as well as for the small, but agile, anti-gentile party." And why? Because in their state, "all the distinctions pertaining to religion, race, and creed were obliterated and one law was promulgated for Jew and non-Jew alike. This law brought to the Jewish state a stream of non-Jewish immigrants, who have benefited the land and who have inter-married with the indigenous Jews."[3]

The accused defends his libelous article in court: "I am a Jew, a native of Eretz Israel. Born on this sacred Canaanite land in Hebron, site of the resting place of the Patriarch Abraham, man of God, and therefore I am tied to our land through stronger links than those cosmopolitans." But the prosecutor responds to this anti-goyish tirade by reaffirming the nation's concept of its tolerant, pluralistic nature and demands, "in the name of Herzl and Nordau," a severe sentence. This request having been granted, the masses rush to the streets to celebrate the victory of tolerance and "congratulate each other upon the demise of anti-Gentileness."

Not only secular Zionists adhered to these concepts. Religious Zionists, too—spurning or forgetting theological difficulties—subscribed to these lofty ideals. Israel's Declaration of Independence takes for granted such ideals and is couched in liberal and universalist terms. Indeed, given the constant war and prolonged siege, utterly unforeseen by the Zionist founders, Israel has fared remarkably well in its treatment of the large Arab minority residing within its borders. It has certainly avoided the pitfalls into which older democracies fell in time of national emergency through their treatment of "alien minorities." When one compares the treatment of Americans of Japanese origin by the United States, safely protected from warfare and sabotage by two vast oceans, with the way vulnerable Israel deals with its strongly nationalist Arab community, the Israeli record, even if tarnished and blemished in places, still shines.

However, we are dealing here not with Israel's record but with the resurgence of religious and nationalist chauvinism within the country, a chauvinism which, at least in theory, is aimed not only against the world outside but also against the non-Jews within. The Orthodox religious establishment, while not identifying itself wholly with such extreme views, has failed to disassociate itself from the new mood. The newly emerging fundamentalism seeks to apply ancient laws not only with regard to the title to the Land of Israel but also with regard to non-Jewish minorities living in this land. These are seen by the new religious militants, at best, as entitled to limited rights; at worst, as devoid of any right, suspect automatically of disloyalty, meriting only censure and punishment. While the openly racist, anti-Arab sentiment of the notorious Meir Kahane is shared only by a fringe group (a handful of fanatics made up mainly of new Orthodox immigrants from America) a much wider circle of religious personalities, including rabbis associated with Gush Emunim and the army's religious service, expresses views which seek to place Israel's non-Jewish citizens in an inferior position, ascribing to them all the sins and faults which Jewish tradition ascribed to its oppressors. That such attitudes are the very antithesis of Zionist thinking—an inverted mirror-image to the utopian mirror-image of Herzl and his associates—cannot be doubted. A return to a pre-Zionist frame of mind and a regression into a contemporary application of medieval dicta constitute the very negation of Jewish national revival. It seeks, whether consciously or not, to take the Jews back to the ghetto, albeit an armed one, from which both Emancipation and Zionism sought to free them.

But the new regression runs into difficulties even within its own theological terms. The rules laid down in the pre-Emancipation era were rooted in the very reality of a subjugated minority. Thus, rabbinical courts were forbidden by the Jewish sages from hearing gentile witnesses because they were afraid that under the hostile and alien regime, Jewish witnesses would be intimidated by the presence of such a witness and would be afraid to give evidence contradicting the Gentile's word. This illustrates the clear nexus between Jewish helplessness and the rabbinical attitude to the non-Jew. To apply such a ruling in Israel, where the Jews are the ruling power, as Chief Rabbi Goren did in one instance, is to fly in the face of the very *ratio decidendi* of the old rulings. But this is merely one instance out of many similar decisions: Jews were enjoined, in old sources, from associating with non-Jews for fear they would fall prey to a trap laid against them; it is forbidden to sell a non-Jew a prayer shawl lest it be used by a Gentile to masquerade as a Jew and thus enable him to murder unsuspecting Jews. Scores of rabbinical decisions are thus linked with the reality of life as a persecuted minority and were founded upon justified Jewish fears. But these antiquated rulings have little to do with the State of Israel which came into being to end these very fears and in which it is the non-Jews who are a minority.

Jewish sovereignty has demolished the foundation of a ghetto-inspired outlook. There is a vast difference between academic scribblings avenging Jewish honor in the Pale of Settlement and any attempt to enforce them in a state where Jews wield the power. The first is an understandable exercise in hopeless academic revenge; the second is an unforgivable resort to force and bigotry. Anyone who claims, as many of the newly annointed sages do, that this is authentic Judaism because one can quote supportive ancient authorities fails not only to realize what Zionism is all about but also to understand the very nature of Jewish thought. This new type of fundamentalist Judaism is nothing more than a caricature of an ancient, pluralistic civilization.

But another element makes this caricature even more abhorrent. In Jewish tradition, the seclusion of Jews from the outside world—achieved through Halachic injunctions—had a deeply religious significance: The Jews, the sanctified tribe, the true followers of Mosaic Law, had to be severed from a heathen, semipagan society. The chasm separated holy and unholy, the keepers of the Covenant and those who were not a party to it. The Covenant, and all the laws and rituals emanating from it, defined the very scope of Judaism and as they passed from generation to generation, their obligatory force was never doubted by the devout and the observant. Separation from the gentile world had its ethical purpose.

The rise of secular Judaism and the secular Jewish state has radically altered that equation between observance and exclusiveness. To apply the old rules distinguishing between the sacred and the profane to one of the most secular societies in the West is a travesty of Jewish ethos.

The new religious chauvinism therefore is absurd and contradicts the one clear message which Jewish nationalism proclaims. It does serve one useful purpose. Through the xenophobic new religious Right, one may easily define the two diametrically opposed lessons to be drawn from Jewish history: one holds that the memory of Jewish suffering should lead to a humanistic, universalist approach emphasizing the dangers of intolerance and racism; this is the lesson embodied in the oft-repeated biblical reminders that the Jews were brought "out of the land of Egypt, out of the house of bondage," and that consequently, they were enjoined, "love ye therefore the stranger, for ye were strangers in the land of Egypt."

The other lesson seeks revenge for past sufferings, and beckons the Jews, now that they have their state, to hunt with the wolves and—invoking the injunction to remember the Amalekites—seeks to apply rules of exclusiveness laid down in totally different circumstances.

The rise of religious and nationalist militancy in Israel was nurtured by a sense of internal disappointment with the accomplishments of Zionism. Indeed, anyone who peruses the history of Zionism, examining its unique achievements and dramatic failings, will be aware of the gap between lofty ideals and harsh reality. Zionism was conceived through the marriage of utopia and revolution but its formative years were characterized by a bloody war, and its initiation rites involved a cruel awakening from adolescent dreams. The visions of yesteryear fell on the rocky ground of a new, more problematic, less idealistic society.

Israel, despite its social record, will not lead the world. Jews do not flock to the open gates of their state. The flame of anti-Semitism, which after World War II seemed to be flickering on its way to extinction, has again flared up, fueled by an

anti-Israel mood. This sense of disillusionment is often verbal-
ized in emphatic terms. Gershom Schocken, editor of *Ha'aretz*,
Israel's leading and independent daily wrote:

It did not dawn on the founders of Zionism that the existence of the
Jewish state would be dependent on the constant economic assistance
of the Jews of the Diaspora. The aim of Zionism was to put an end to
Exile and not to establish a state which would be its protégé. If Herzl
would have known that the Jewish state would incorporate only a
fifth of world Jewry and that its political status would be dependent
on "the Jewish vote" in the United States, it is safe to assume that he
would have relinquished the Zionist idea as a means of solving the
Jewish problem and would have reverted to his initial idea of massive
conversion to Christianity.[4]

And the chief rabbi of Britain's Jews, Dr. Imannuel Jakobovits, criticizes secular Zionism, which "had led our people to
believe that if we only had a state of our own we would nor-
malize the Jewish condition." This, states Dr. Jakobovits, "is
now shattered, idle as it always was for religious Jews whose
love of Zion was not generated by persecution or the desire for
normalcy." And the chief rabbi goes further and draws an analogy between the "fallacy" of secular Zionism and the German
Reform Movement in the nineteenth century:

[that] movement sought to achieve equality for the Jew through *individual assimilation*. . . . and came to infinite grief in the very country
where it was to bring us salvation. . . . Let us beware lest trust in the
false promise of salvation by *national assimilation* would lead. . . . to
a debacle of like proportions.[5]

These strong words echo even stronger feelings—all stemming from the sense of a dream frustrated, a vision denied, an
opportunity lost.

Yet, one is entitled to adopt a more realistic attitude, to
measure Israel's record not only against the utopian aspirations
of her founding fathers but as a self-contained epic, full of its
own grief and glory. Utopia—including the predicted end of

anti-Semitism—was the prime mover of the resettlement of the Promised Land, but after the trials and tribulations which befell the Jewish people in this century, it cannot be retained as an exclusive yardstick; nor can Herzl's expectations, in pre-Nazi Europe, to see the total demise of anti-Semitism be taken as anything more than a pious wish, now that we know how deeply rooted are religious and tribal instincts. If Herzl could not have conceived of the coexistence of Jew-hatred and Jewish sovereignty, neither could he—nor, for that matter, anybody else—have foreseen the resurgence of religious warfare in Northern Ireland and similar cravings for ethnic separatism in the very heart of Europe. The failure of the Zionist political naiveté in the Middle East is part of a more general failure to predict the most rudimentary trends which were destined to have their imprint on our century, just as the failure of total socialism in Israel must be seen in the wider context of a god that failed. To judge Israel—alone of all societies—by the climate of opinion pervading a buried world is an exercise in futility, even if, as this author firmly believes, Israel must take a political road whose very direction was mapped out by the founding fathers.

Indeed, a more pragmatic, less idealistic and consequently less apocalyptic, attitude is necessary in order to bring Israel back to the past course which led her to unassailable peaks. Israel may have failed to gather in the exiles, but it has given Jews everywhere a new focus of attention and pride not weakened by periodical pangs of anxiety. Moreover, Israel may have not stemmed anti-Semitism but it has forced both Jew and non-Jew to recognize the true nature of the object of this estrangement. Dr. David Hartman, scholar and Orthodox rabbi, elucidated this point:

The profound sense of isolation and spiritual loneliness experienced by the Jewish people in the Diaspora stemmed from our not being heard in the way we hear ourselves. Christianity saw us as an anachronism, as a pariah in history. Because the intimate relationship between peoplehood and spirituality in Judaism was incomprehensible to others, we found ourselves put into a straitjacket, not able to make ourselves and our relationship to God intelligible to others. . . . Now Israel stands before the world and announces publicly that peoplehood, nationhood, and spirituality are inextricably bound with each other, that Judaism cannot be understood without recognizing its peoplehood aspirations. In this sense, Israel has healed anti-Semitism by forcing the world to listen to us and hear us as we hear ourselves, and not in alien categories. . . . Israel's existence has liberated both Christians and Jews to listen with profound sensitivity to each other's particularity.[6]

A more pragmatic attitude, avoiding the exclamation marks of both fervent vision and dark despair, means something else: a sense of modesty about the aims and targets of the Jewish state. Indeed, when one surveys the history of Zionist thought, one must be impressed by the duality which inheres in the very concept of normalization. On the one hand, there are the lofty ideas and the impressive deeds seeking to turn the Jewish state into a model state, a leader of nations, a pacesetter on the road to progress; on the other hand, one is also struck by a certain spiritual shallowness of the vision itself; secular messianism may have sounded an apt term—and the semireligious revolutionary fervor was certainly there—but Zionist thinking is bereft of true religiosity. The men who gave expression to the Zionist idea and made it come true did not see in Jewish nationalism a means of spiritual salvation. They wanted to establish a progressive Jewish society, but they did not seek to give the Jews new tablets of the Law. Theirs was a down-to-earth wish: to give the Jews a home—a house, not a Temple— so that they would be able to live in it in decency, preserve old traditions, develop their old-new language, create their new culture, continue their quarrels and serve as a welcoming shelter to their suffering brethren. They wanted the new dwellers of the old, forsaken home to become new liberated Jews and to act as orderly good neighbors among the older members of the family of nations. Herzl and his followers needed neither a new Temple, nor an alernative to old altars. It was not a cultural void or a spiritual need which drove them to the newly espoused idea. The claim to the Land of Israel—neglected and partially unpossessed—was made not because of its religious sanctity, but because this was the only home which Jews ever knew, from which they had been ejected, and to whose memory they have always clung. It was, in short, the only house they could call their home. The early Zionists were not conscious of the fury with which the Arab occupants would reject the return of the old owners. But this rejection, as well as the boycott of the whole neighborhood, cannot alter the nature of the house which Zionism has built: a home and not a temple, a secular nation and not a sacred tribe, a good neighbor waiting for feuds to subside, and not a recluse destined and willing to reside alone.

Israel will be measured, and its future will depend, on its will and ability to return to these old truths.

NOTES

Preface

1. *Ma'ariv* (Tel Aviv), August 8, 1982, p. 20.
2. Original letter quoted, parts of which are quoted in the *Jerusalem Post*, August 3, 1982.
3. Letter quoted in *The New York Times*, October 2, 1982, p. 9.
4. *Ha'aretz* (Tel Aviv), August 11, 1982.
5. *Ha'aretz*, July 5, 1982.
6. *Davar* (Tel Aviv), December 31, 1982.
7. The Commission of Inquiry into the Events at the Refugee Camps in Beirut, *Final Report* (Jerusalem, 1983), p. 55. Authorized translation.
8. London *Spectator*, June 19, 1982.
9. *Anti-Defamation League Bulletin* (New York), November 1982, p. 15.
10. *Mesimvrini* (Athens), July 6, 1982.

Chapter 1

1. Ze'ev (Vladimir) Jabotinsky, *Ktavim Tzioni'im Rishonim* [Early Zionist writings] (Jerusalem, 1949), pp. 97–100.
2. *Ktavim* [Writings], ed. B. Katzenelson (Tel Aviv, 1939), p. 59.
3. Y. Becker and S. Shpan, *Mivchar Ha'massah Ha'ivrit* [Selected Hebrew essays] (Tel Aviv, 1945), pp. 68–70.
4. Theodor Herzl, "The Jewish State (1896)," in Arthur Hertzberg, ed., *The Zionist Idea* (New York: Harper Torchbooks, 1966), p. 225.
5. "Die Geuleh" [The Redemption] (1917), quoted by Y. Gorni in *Hatzionut*, ed. D. Carpi, vol. 2 (Tel Aviv, 1971), p. 77.
6. A. Fishman, *Hapo'el Ha'mizrachi* (Tel Aviv, 1979), p. 162.
7. Hertzberg, p. 209.

8. Max Nordau, "Speech to the First Zionist Congress," in Hertzberg, p. 241.

9. T. Herzl, *The Jewish State* (New York: Herzl Press, 1970), p. 110.

10. Ahad Ha'am, *Kol Kitvei* [Collected writings] (Tel Aviv, 1947), pp. 313–20.

11. Ahad Ha'am, p. 286.

12. Jacob Klatzkin, "Boundaries (1914–1921)," in Hertzberg, p. 326.

Chapter 2

1. *Ha'umma Veha'avodah* [The Nation and Labor] (Jerusalem, 1951), pp. 365–67.

2. *The Zionist Idea* (New York: Harper Torchbooks, 1966), pp. 17–18.

3. Theodor Herzl, "The Jewish State (1896)," in Hertzberg, p. 209.

4. *Evidence Submitted to the Palestine Royal Commission* (London, 1937), p. 11.

5. *Poems*, tr. D. Kuselewitz (Tel Aviv, 1978), p. 91.

6. *Kol Kitvei* [Collected writings] vol. 6 (Tel Aviv, 1927), pp. 103–4, 117.

7. *Israeli Stories*, ed. Joel Blocker (New York: Schocken Books, 1962), p. 65.

8. *Ktavim* [Writings] (Haifa, 1971), pp. 154, 219.

9. *Hannah Senesh, Her Life and Diary* (New York: Schocken Books, 1973), p. 115.

10. David Canaani, *Ha'aliyah Hasheniyah Ha'ovedet Vichassah Ladat Velamassoret* [The Second Aliyah and its attitude to religion and tradition] (Tel Aviv, 1976), p. 111.

11. Canaani, p. 87.

12. Quoted from *Hatzionut*, ed. D. Carpi, vol. 2 (Tel Aviv, 1971), p. 89. The article was written in 1917.

13. *Aleph*, June 1951.

14. *Massa Haptichah*, republished in *Reshit Ha'yamim* (Tel Aviv, 1982), p. 152.

15. *Aleph*, June, 1951.

Chapter 3

1. Moses Hess, "Rome and Jerusalem" in Arthur Hertzberg, ed., *The Zionist Idea* (New York: Harper Torchbooks, 1966), p. 129.

2. Ahad Ha'am, *Kol Kitvei* [Collected writings] (Tel Aviv, 1947), p. 408.

3. Ibid., p. 325.

4. Abraham Isaac Kook, "The Rebirth of Israel (1910–1930)," in Hertzberg, p. 425.

5. Judah Leon Magnes, "Like All the Nations? (1930)" in Hertzberg, p. 447.

6. Martin Buber, "Hebrew Humanism" in Hertzberg, p. 459.

7. Joseph Chaim Brenner, *Kol Kitvei* [Collected writings] (Tel Aviv, 1927), p. 259.

8. Micha Joseph Berdichevsky, "Wrecking and Building (1900–1903)," in Hertzberg, p. 293.

9. Jacob Klatzkin, "Boundaries (1914–1921)," in Hertzberg, p. 319.

10. Nachum Syrkin, "The Jewish Problem and the Socialist-Jewish State (1898)," in Hertzberg, p. 350.

11. David Ben Gurion, *Yihud Ve'yiud* [Singularity and destiny], I.D.F. ed. (Tel Aviv, n.d.), p. 13.

12. *Hatzedek Hasotzialisti Vehatzedek Hamishpati Vehamussari Shelanu* [Socialist justice and our moral and legal justice] (Tel Aviv, 1936), p. 110.

13. *Lenivchei Hatkuffah* [On the perplexities of our age] (Jerusalem, 1943), p. 236.

14. *Sefer Matan Torah* (Jerusalem, 1940), p. 106.

Chapter 4

1. *Ktavim Autobiographi'im* [Autobiographical writings] vol. 2 (Jerusalem, 1970), p. 196.

2. *Le'an* [Whither?] (Tel Aviv, n.d.), p. 62.

3. *Chalomot U'milchamot* [Dreams and wars] (Jerusalem, 1975), p. 205.

4. *Ha'aravim Be'eretz-Israel* [The Arabs in the Land of Israel] (Tel Aviv, 1969), pp. 23–24.

5. *An Autobiography* (Tel Aviv, n.d.), p. 53.

6. *Hashiloach*, vol. 17 (Odessa, 1907), pp. 193–206.

7. Theodor Herzl, *Igrot* [Letters] (Jerusalem, 1957), pp. 309–10.

8. A. Karlebach, *Va'adat Ha'chakirah Ha'anglo-Americait Le'inyenei Eretz-Israel* [The Anglo-American Inquiry Commission on Palestine] vol. 2 (Tel Aviv, 1946), p. 675.

9. "Leverur Matzav Ha'falachim" [on the state of the fellahin] 1917, republished in *Anu Ushcheneinu* [We and our neighbors] (Tel Aviv, 1935), pp. 13–25.

10. *Sipurim* [Stories] (Ramat Gan, 1976), p. 65.

11. Shabtai Teveth, *Moshe Dayan* (London and Jerusalem: Weidenfeld and Nicholson, Steimatzky), p. 46.

12. Ze'ev Jabotinsky, *Sipurim* [Stories] (Tel Aviv, 1980), p. 7.

13. *Hashilo'ah*, vol. 27 (Odessa, 1912), p. 508; see also Gideon Ofrat, "The Arab in Israeli Drama," in *The Jerusalem Quarterly*, 11 (Spring 1979): 70.

14. *Hashilo'ah*, vol. 17 (Odessa, 1907), p. 574.

15. "Massa Arav," in Joseph Chaim Brenner's *Hameorer* (London, 1907), p. 278.

16. *Nedudei Amshi Hashomer* (Jerusalem and Tel Aviv, 1929).

17. Y. Porat, *The Emergence of the Palestinian-Arab National Movement, 1918–1928* (London, 1974), p. 68.

18. M. Assaf, *Hayechassim bein Aravim Veyehudim Be'eretz-Israel* [The relations between Arabs and Jews in Eretz Israel] (Tel Aviv, 1970), p. 180.

19. *Minutes of the Palestine Royal Commission* (London, 1936), p. 236.

20. *Dvarim Bego* [Explications and implications; writings on Jewish heritage and renaissance] (Tel Aviv, 1975), p. 115–16.

21. *Ma'ariv*, September 9, 1976.

22. *Me'chayeinu*, no. 11 (1922), reissued by the Archives of Labor (Tel Aviv, 1971). The bulletin was published in Kibbutz Ein Harod in the 1920s.

Chapter 5

1. Reported in *Haboker* (Tel Aviv daily), December 7, 1942.

2. *Ha'aretz* (Tel Aviv), February 2, 1945. Ben Gurion's words created a storm of protest both at the Council and in the Yiddish press in America.

3. David Ben Gurion, *Yihud Ve'yiud* [Singularity and destiny] I.D.F. ed. (Tel Aviv, n.d.), pp. 40–42.

4. A. Ben Asher, *Yechassei Chutz, 1948–1953* [Foreign relations, 1948–1953] (Tel Aviv, 1956), p. 9.

5. *Israel Umashber Hatzivilizatziah Hama'aravit* [Israel and the crisis of western civilization] (Tel Aviv, 1972), p. 11.

Chapter 6

1. *An Autobiography* (New York: Random House, 1977), p. 392.

2. *Hatsofeh* (Tel Aviv), October 19, 1971.

3. *Ma'ariv* (Tel Aviv), July 13, 1973.
4. *Ma'ariv*, September 13, 1973.
5. *Ma'ariv*, May 6, 1973.
6. *La'ohavim et ha'aviv* (Tel Aviv, 1981), p. 32.
7. H. C. 58/68 Shalit v. Minister of Interior, *Selected Judgments of the Supreme Court of Israel, Special Volume* (Jerusalem, 1971), p. 35, (in English).
8. *Ha'aretz* (Tel Aviv), April 30, 1973.
9. *Ha'aretz*, December 8, 1967.
10. *Ha'aretz*, April 12, 1968.
11. *Ha'aretz*, August 8, 1980.
12. *Davar* (Tel Aviv), March 31, 1980.
13. "The Exposed American Jew," *Commentary*, 59 (June 1975): 25, 27–8.
14. Amos Oz, "A Late Love," in *Unto Death* (New York: Harcourt Brace, 1975), pp. 156–58.
15. Chanoch Bartov, *Dado*, vol. 1 (Tel Aviv, 1978), p. 261. The English version (Tel Aviv, 1981) does not include this passage.
16. "The Historical Significance of the Holocaust," *The Jerusalem Quarterly*, 1 (Fall 1976): 36, 59–60.
17. *Davar*, October 5, 1979.

Chapter 7

1. *Ha'aretz* (Tel Aviv), April 16, 1968.
2. *Ha'aretz*, September 25, 1968.
3. *Ha'ma'alot Mima'makim* [Up from the depths] (Jerusalem, 1974), pp. 42–43.
4. *Machshavot* [Thoughts] (Benei Brak, 1975), pp. 7–8.
5. (London Weidenfeld and Nicholson 1978) p. 7.
6. *Petahim*, 47–48 (September 1979): 66. Quarterly of Jewish thought.
7. *Deot*, 45 (1976): 333. A journal of religious academics.
8. Ibid.
9. *Niv Ha'midrashiyah*, 11 (1974): 159.
10. *Yehiel*, pp. 6, 8.
11. *Niv Ha'midrashiyah*, p. 159.
12. *Bat Kol*, February 26, 1980. Bar Ilan University students' journal.
13. *Lentivot Israel*, (Jerusalem, 1967), pp. 118–19.
14. *Ha'aretz*, May 9, 1976.
15. *Nekudah*, 52 (September 1982): 8. A journal of the settlements in Judea, Samaria and Gaza.

16. A paid advertisement published in several journals.
17. From an interview in *Yediot Ahronot*, June 18, 1976.
18. *Leshem Shinui* (Tel Aviv) October 1976, p. 4. Shinui movement monthly.
19. *Ha'aretz*, September 21, 1979.

Chapter 8

1. "Le'iladim," in *Yediot Ahronot*, October 8, 1976.
2. *Ha'aretz* (Tel Aviv), November 11, 1946.
3. *Mikan Umikan* (1911) in *Ktavim* [Writings], vol. 2 (Tel Aviv, 1946), p. 336.
4. "Generational Units and Intergenerational Relations in Israeli Politics" in *Israel: A Developing Society* (The Netherlands: Van Gorcum, Assen, 1980), p. 168.
5. *Ha'aretz* (Tel Aviv), June 6, 1952.
6. *With His Own Hands*, tr. J. Shacter (Jerusalem, 1970), p. 1.
7. Zvi Luz, *Metziut Veadam Bassifrut Ha'eretz-Israelit* [Reality and the individual in Eretz Israeli literature] (Tel Aviv, 1970), p. 103.
8. *The First Million Sabras* (New York: Hart Publishing, 1970), p. 11.
9. Quoted in S. B. Beit-Zvi, *Ha'tzionut Hapost-Ugandit Bemashber Hasho'ah* [Post-Ugandan Zionism in the crucible of the Holocaust] (Tel Aviv, 1977), p. 386.
10. *Keshet* (Tel Aviv) (Summer 1968): 128.
11. *Moto Shel Uri Peled* (Tel Aviv, 1971), p. 9.
12. Amiram Amitai, *Milchemet Hasheluliut* (Tel Aviv, 1968).
13. *Ziyunim Ze Lo Hakol* (Tel Aviv, 1979), p. 116.
14. Quoted in I. Yaoz-Kest, *Hatfissah Ha'neo-Yehudit* [The neo-Jewish attitude] (Tel Aviv, 1974), p. 11.
15. "Moti Ba li Peta," in *Makom Shel Esh* (Tel Aviv, 1975), p. 84. Author's translation.
16. "Rak Ben Essrim," in *Shdemot*, literary journal of the kibbutz movement. no. 54 (Tel Aviv, 1974), p. 64. Author's translation.
17. "Ribono Shel Olam," in *Shdemot*, no. 53 (Tel Aviv, 1974), p. 127. Author's translation; for another translation, see *Lines Cut: Posthumous Poems of Four Young Israelis* (Tel Aviv, 1981), p. 65.
18. *Siman Kri'ah*, 11 (May 1980): 87.
19. *Ha'aretz*, August 20, 1982.
20. *Lo Lagiborim Ha'milchamah* (Tel Aviv, 1971), p. 104.
21. *Mishlei Bakbukim* (Tel Aviv, 1975), p. 95.

22. *Sha'ar Knissah, Sha'ar Yetsi'ah* [Entrance gate, exit gate] (Tel Aviv, 1981), p. 61. Author's translation.
23. Dahn, Ben Arnotz, p. 120.
24. *Ha'aretz*, December 13, 1978.
25. Beit-Zvi, p. 377.
26. Ibid.

Chapter 9

1. *Ma'ariv* (Tel Aviv), February 29, 1980.
2. Ahad Ha'am quoted in Arthur Hertzberg, ed., *The Zionist Idea* (New York: Harper Torchbooks, 1966), p. 71.

Chapter 10

1. Quoted in Jacob Katz, *Exclusiveness and Tolerance* (New York: Schocken Books, 1962), pp. 185, 187–88.
2. Theodor Herzl, *Old-New Land* [Altneuland] tr. L. Levensohn (New York: Bloch Publishing and Herzl Press, 1960), p. 139.
3. *Die Welt*, 1898, vol. 2, nos. 13, 15, 17, and 18.
4. *Ha'aretz* (Tel Aviv), September 10, 1980.
5. *The Holocaust, Contemporary Jewry, Zionism Today, Spiritual Leadership—A Call for Reappraisal* (London: Office of the Chief Rabbi, 1979), pp. 6–7.
6. *Ammi, no. 11* (Jerusalem: World Union for Progressive Judaism, pp. 10–11.

INDEX

Abdul Hamid, Sultan, 54
Abraham, xii, 38, 100, 106, 108, 113, 119
Adenauer, Konrad, 74
Afghanistan, 52
Africa, 79, 159
agriculture, political importance of, 11, 26–28, 48, 94, 109–110
Ahad Ha'am (Asher Zvi Ginsberg), 13, 17–19, 39–40, 74, 169
  on blood libels, 85
  on Jewish uniqueness, 164–165
  Zionism of, 39, 72
Alexander II, Czar of Russia, 14
Ali Ja'abri, Sheikh, 100
Al'Khaldy, Yousuf, 55
Allah Karim (Orloff-Arieli), 58–59
Allon, Yigal, 100, 107
Altneuland (Herzl), 11, 13, 53–54, 74, 175–176
Amalekites, biblical references to, xii, 116, 157, 180
American Council for Judaism, 71–72
Amiel, Moshe A., 48
Amital, Yehuda, 104–105, 118
am segula ("treasure nation"), *see* chosenness
Anglo-American Inquiry Commission, 55
Anshlag, Yehuda, 48–49
Anti-Defamation League, xvi–xvii
"Anti-Gentileness in Zion" (Behar), 176–177
anti-Semitism, 8, 21–23, 39, 50, 80–92, 162–163

anti-Zionism linked with, xviii, 80–89, 158–164
Arab adoption of, 63–65, 83, 161
continuity of, in Diaspora, 162–163
intellectuals' acquiescence to, 14
irrationality of, 162
medieval, 86–87, 173–174
modern, xvi–xix, 180–181
nineteenth-century resurgence of, 8, 14, 86–88, 94, 175
Zionism as liberation from, xix, 8–12, 65, 69, 87, 90, 115, 175–177, 181–183
Zionist explanation of, 21–23, 72
Appelfeld, Aharon, 138
"Arabia Decepta," 158
Arabs:
  anti-Semitism adopted by, 63–65, 83, 161
  economic power of, 79, 81, 83, 158–160
  European appeasement of, 69, 83
  fundamentalist view of, 116, 157
  in Hebrew literature, 59–61, 139, 142
  in Israel and occupied territories, 100–103, 108, 160, 177
  Jewish overtures rejected by, 62–68, 86, 129, 164, 184
  labor Zionism and, 55–56, 60, 62–63
  nationalism among, 54, 61–62, 161
  Nazis among, 152
  Zionism's benefits to, 54–56, 63
  Zionist alignment with, 52–61